To my HERO
our HERO
Thank you
Harold.

A Boy and a Book:

Overcoming Obstacles through the Magic of Reading

By Dr. Harold Fernandez

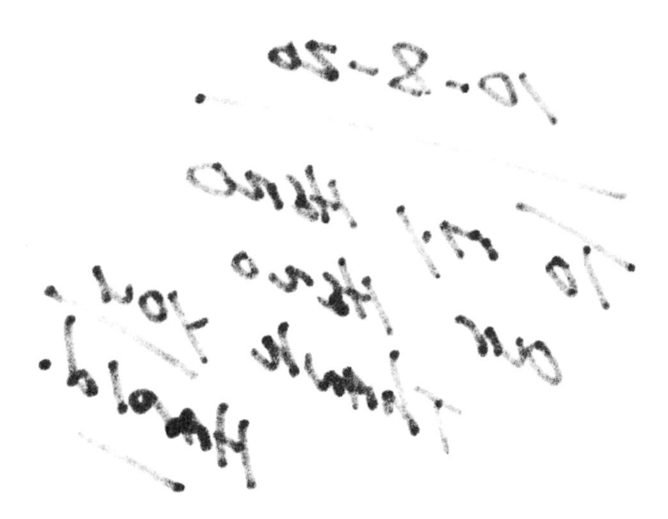

A Boy and a Book

Independently published

Edited by Joanne Asala, Brooks Becker, Jasmine Fernandez
Cover and interior design by Asya Blue

Published in the United States

For information visit www.haroldfernandez.com

ISBN 9780578723310 (paperback)
ISBN 9780578723327 (e-book)

Contents

Dedication

To my *Abuelitas*, Rosa and Alicia,
for their infinite love

and

To my parents, Angela and Alberto,
for bringing me to America

and

To every girl and boy
who has a dream burning in their heart

and

To the magic of books
for giving me a life serving others

Acknowledgments

"Mostly, your talk was moving because it was sincere and heartfelt. What a great feeling it must be to look into this crowd of students and reflect back to the day you first arrived in the United States. And for us, what a wonderful feeling it is to see this American Dream reflected back. Thank you."

—Joy Anajovich (bilingual social studies teacher at Brentwood High School, NY)

"We cannot thank you enough for speaking with our students last week. Your story is one that all should hear. Our students were very inspired. They were talking about your presentation in their classes. I personally, went home to tell my daughter the 3 steps to success and I have been enforcing it. Again, we appreciate you taking the time out of your busy schedule!"

—Abby Archdeacon (school counselor, Westbury High School, NY)

Over the course of writing this manuscript, my inspiration has been the students and other young adults that I have met when I give presentations at schools or at celebrations for Hispanic heritage month, graduations, or keynote addresses. In their eyes and faces, I see their struggles and it reminds me of the same journey that I endured on my road to a career helping others. I would like to thank them for giving me the opportunity to come into their lives.

I also want to thank Mr. Michael Dowling (CEO of Northwell Health), Dr. Alan Hartman (my boss and friend), Dr. James Taylor (friend, colleague, and mentor) and the entire Community Relations Division at Northwell Health for giving me the opportunity and the platform to be an active participant in their successful medical career day program at many of the schools in Long Island where I present my story, "From Immigrant to Cardiac Surgeon," in Spanish and English. This has allowed me the privilege to meet hundreds of young people who dream of improving their lives through an education, but who often may feel overwhelmed by the challenges they face.

In addition, a special heartfelt thanks to Mr. Alberto Minota for giving me the space over the last seven years at White Plains High School to speak with his students. My love and appreciation also to the many leaders of the civic and scholastic organizations here in Long Island, but especially Osman Canales; Dafny Irizarry; Pilar Moya; Pilar Delgado; Margarita Espada; Ed Roldan; Olga El Sehamy; Elizabeth Custodio; George Siberon; Rev. Allan Ramirez; Dr. David Sperling (and his entire team at the Dream Foundation); Margarita Grasing; Lynda Perdomo-Ayala; and, of course, Dr. Allecia McLeod, who invites me every year for her medical career day at the Reed Middle School in Central Islip. I can just imagine how tired you all are of hearing this story so many times. So, thank you for your patience and also for your dedication to improving the lives of our young students and for giving me the opportunity to make a minute contribution to their education. In each conference, my goal has been to motivate, but I often find that it is I who feels inspired and energized after meeting them and hearing about some of the monumental obstacles that many of them are facing. I hope that in return, I can inspire them by sharing the story of how through the magic of books, all dreams are possible.

Finally, all my love to my wife, Sandra; my daughter, Jasmine; and my dear son, Brandon, for their love, patience, and never-ending support in each of my crazy endeavors, which often end up stealing time away from the special moments we have together.

Prologue

Yes, there were many times that I felt in my heart like a wimpy kid, overwhelmed with the obstacles and challenges in front of me. I wanted to give up. I did not believe in myself. Perhaps this was related to my status as a new undocumented immigrant in America starting all over again in a new country, without knowing the language, not having friends or even the legal permission to be here without hiding. Or perhaps this was related to the fears inside my head that the other students were better prepared and more intelligent than I was. Yes, there were many times that I was consumed by all these thoughts, and in my heart, after all, I felt like a wimpy kid. But in this world of darkness and fears, I was able to find refuge, hope, and light within the magic of books.

Today, as an adult, I no longer feel wimpy. I am a heart surgeon—a confident one—a career made possible because of my lifelong dedication to educating and training myself to the best of my abilities. After many years at the world's most prestigious universities, I now have the privilege and honor to help my patients by getting into their chests and fixing their hearts. But don't worry, this book is not about heart surgery, or even medicine. This book is about something much simpler. This is a story of falling in love with books. It's a story about how this simple idea transformed my life and gave me all the tools that I needed to succeed in my career as a healer. I am confident that a love for books and reading can transform the life of any boy or girl who may feel like a wimpy kid and is trying to make his or her own dreams a reality, too.

You see, when I was thirteen years old, it appeared as if I wasn't going to be very successful in life. The odds were not in my favor. This was when I found myself stranded on a tiny island in the Bahamas waiting for a boat to pick me up and bring me to America. I arrived here after a perilous journey on this small boat that snuck into America through a corner of the Bermuda Triangle—all to come and join my parents in America as another undocumented immigrant.

The complex world of American schools brought me many challenges I hadn't anticipated. Still, I worked hard to overcome all obstacles and, in the process, discovered that I actually had an advantage. I had learned something as a kid growing up in the turbulence of Medellín, Colombia. It was my passion for books and an education. And it was this love for books that gave me the edge to succeed in school, including at Princeton University and Harvard Medical School. In this epic story, I will describe my own journey into the Ivy League, with the hope that it inspires, motivates, and points the way for other young readers toward finding inspiration and the motivation to change their own lives and conquer their own demons. And it all starts with the power of a book and a love for reading.

Presently, I don't spend all my time in an operating room. One of my favorite activities involves getting out and sharing my story with young students. My message is simple. I tell them that success in school is within the reach of every student, and it is directly related to how serious they are about reading books. I remind them that the kids who become professional soccer players spend all their time with a soccer ball. Similarly, the kids who become professional basketball players spend all their time with a basketball. These kids do not make an excuse about not having a soccer ball. The ones who really want it go out and make their own soccer ball. These kids do not go and tell their parents that they can't play because they don't have shoes. These kids go out and play barefoot. I know this because I have seen it with my own eyes as old friends of mine would play outside in the streets of Medellín's Barrio Antioquia, where I grew up, without shoes because they could not afford them. By the same token, success in school depends on how much time is spent with books.

Unfortunately, what I have seen in the eyes of many of the young people I meet is that they have already given up. In their hearts, I know that many of them may feel as I did, like a wimpy kid. In their minds, they have convinced themselves that they are not good enough. Some of them have been told by their friends and sometimes even by their own parents that they are not good enough to follow their dreams. Many of them are just waiting for the most opportune moment to leave school and find a job. One of the reasons why many students have lost motivation is that no one has ever taken the time to teach them the power of books, an education, or the importance of believing in themselves. There were many nights that I felt like giving up. There were many failures, and there were many people who did not believe that I could make my dream of becoming a doctor a reality. Yet I was able to change my life because I learned how to love books.

It is very simple to just go out and tell students that they must fall in love with books. However, this is easier said than done. And it's why I have decided to also make this story an instructional guide on how to get it done. Within the narrative of my story, I will give practical advice on how to study and how to read. I feel that the better of a reader that you are, the more you will enjoy the stories you come across and the more you will fall in love with the books that contain them. This was certainly my own personal experience. And I can attest that it works because it worked for me at Princeton University, at Harvard Medical School, and at MIT. It will also work for any student or anyone trying to succeed in school.

Somewhere tonight, a young boy or girl will be sitting down by a desk struggling to learn and succeed in school. Or perhaps another young person will be struggling to find something positive in life that will make them feel good about themselves. Or perhaps that young person is trying to fall asleep but can't because they are struggling with their own demons, problems with discipline in school and feelings of being overwhelmed, isolated, and helpless. If this is the case, this is the perfect book for them or even their parents. I have put my heart and soul into the pages of this book to help those students. I have written the book that I wish I could have read when I was consumed with fear. I am pleased to know that if this book can change the life of one person, it will be worth the time and effort that I have put into it.

This is a story of love, inspiration, overcoming obstacles, and triumph at the highest levels of American academic institutions. But most importantly, this is a true story of how a young boy who felt like a wimpy kid was able to change his life through the power of books, which gave him the confidence that he needed to overcome all obstacles. Yes, it is that simple. Even in today's vast highly digital world of computers, cell phones, social media, video games, and many other distractions, there is no substitute for the infinite, life-changing power of falling in love with books. I invite you to come into my world and discover how I fell in love with them and how this simple idea has brought me to a fulfilling life as a healer.

"If there is a book that you want to read, but it hasn't been written yet, then you must write it."
— Toni Morrison

1
The Green Sofa

"There isn't a skill more powerful than being able to read well."
—Harold Fernandez

"My love, books will change your life," my mama whispered with a soft, caring voice as I struggled to stay awake.

Yawning and rubbing my eyes, I replied, "Yes, Mama. Yes, Mama, but I am so tired. Can I please go to bed now? Please, Mama!"

My mother, Angela, had been reading to me all day from a picture book collection with large letters and colorful drawings. The books had many drawings of animals in bright colors and were filled with breath-taking stories of an imaginary world that, while it kept my attention and focus on the paper, carried me to magnificent places filled with magic and adventure. Each turn of the page was a mysterious new journey. The scent of the paper and the sensation of its texture on my skin as I softly ran my fingers over the pictures was simply memorable. I loved these moments with Mama, but tonight I was so tired. It was already dark outside. As I glanced out into the courtyard, I could just make out the faint rays of moonlight entering through the patio. My mother wanted me to learn how to read quickly and to be ready for school. In Barrio Antioquia, my hometown in Medellín, Colombia, I did not have access to a kindergarten year, so Mama took it upon herself to teach me how to read so I would be ready for first grade. I was seven years old. In just a few months, I would start the greatest journey of my life as a first grader.

But there was another, more urgent reason that my mother was in a rush to teach me. As we lay together on the green, rounded sofa the shape of a gigantic drum, my mother said, "Just a few more minutes, my love. You must really work hard so that you can impress Papa when he returns from America." Yes, this was the real reason Mama was in such a rush. I knew how important this was because she spoke every day as if Papa was coming home the next day, or even that night. The truth was that my father, Alberto, had been away for just over three years, and no one really knew when he was coming back. Nevertheless, Mama wanted to make sure that if my father entered through the front door, he would discover that his eldest son was a good reader and ready for school. This was very important for them because both of my parents had left school at a very early age. My father hadn't even finished first grade, and my mother had only made it through third grade. They did not want the same fortune for their kids. They wanted something better.

As I tried to concentrate and read some more, we were suddenly interrupted by the uproar of my younger brother, Byron, running through the front entrance and into the long, open patio where the green sofa was located. Byron was not alone. He never was! He was running furiously and had a broomstick placed between his legs, pretending that it was a horse. There were several other dirty and smelly kids with makeshift horse toys following him. They were all playing and having a good time. They were playing their favorite game, pretending they were Indians and cowboys. I looked Mama in her eyes and said, "Come on, Mama, please let me go and play with them. I really want to go and play. Please, Mama." Angela raised her voice, and with a firm reply said, "I thought you said you were sleepy? No, no, my love. We have work to do."

As I glanced at Byron running and playing with several of the street kids from the neighborhood, I envied my younger brother. Although I treasured this time with Mama and the stories, I very much preferred to be the one playing with these neighborhood kids, not the one glued to this green sofa trying to learn how to read. I then looked into my mother's beautiful green eyes again and asked, "Why me, Mama? Why do I have to be here learning how to read? Why can't we just wait until I start school, so I can learn how to read with the other kids?" She hastily answered, "No, Harold, we can't wait. You have to learn how to read soon. Remember, your father will be coming home any day." I felt an urge to speak my mind and tell her, "No, Mama, he is not coming back. He has forgotten about us!" But I held back. This was not the first time I had thought this, and I knew how sad and upset Mama would be if I said it aloud. The return of my father was a very delicate subject that we did not often discuss in the open. I just turned my head and put all my attention on the pictures and the book one more time. This was a way for me to escape the pain of having Papa so far away. Despite being so tired, I was slowly developing a love for books.

That green sofa held a special place in my heart. I spent many moments there with Mama learning how to read. This was where she would tell me stories and explain events related to our long separation from Papa. With many dreams in his heart, my father had left for America when I was just four years old. I had faint memories of his face and voice and the love we shared, but I also had many questions. My mother would take these moments to share stories with us and show us many photos and read letters that Papa would send from America. Photos of places like the Statue of Liberty, Coney Island, the Empire State Building, Atlantic City, the Twin Towers, the hanging bridges, and the beautiful streets of New York City. In my young mind, America seemed an amazing paradise, like the cities in my imagination as I read the books with my mother. A place of magic where everything is possible.

This sofa was also the place where I would often come to lie down and cry and beg the Lord to keep my father safe, and to please bring him home soon so we could be together as a family again. On the wall right next to the sofa was a picture of Papa. Each time we thought that Mama was excessively strict or we had arguments, I would run to this sofa and throw myself on top and yell out loud to my father, "Please come back, Papa. Please return. We need you here."

In many ways, Byron, two years younger than me, was a much livelier, friendlier, and more playful kid. He had big, round black eyes and a contagious smile that he carried with him permanently. Never still, he was always running, causing a riot with his band of friends. He always seemed to be surrounded by a multitude of kids his age from around the block who would follow him everywhere, including into the house, where he would often bring them into the kitchen and give them food, or candy, or *aguapanela* (sugar-cane water) from the big container that Mama always had on the kitchen counter. Within his group of friends, Byron was always in the lead. Many of these kids were very poor and had dirty clothes, and some of them didn't even have shoes. Their parents were very poor. Mama was a gentle soul and did not mind all these dirty kids running around the house with Byron. Even more important, tonight, Mama was a woman with a mission, and I was her assignment. She was determined that I would learn how to read. So we continued word by word until my lips could just barely open and my head was flinging forward as if I had been knocked out in a fight. "My love, wake up, wake up." She tried one more time. But I was totally asleep, and she had to carry me to bed. She gently tucked me in and gave me a kiss, and put the sign of the cross on my forehead, softly whispering the Lord's Prayer over me: "God our Father, hallowed be thy name..."

"Oh God, please protect my sons from all that is evil and dangerous."

As she walked out of my bedroom, she had a glow in the center of her light-green eyes and a gentle smile of satisfaction. She thought that I was making good progress. This made her happy. She was content that if Papa walked through the front door that night, he would approve of the fine work she had done teaching me how to read. This inner satisfaction only lasted briefly as her joy was interrupted again by the loud noises of Byron and his band of friends running into the house, yelling and pretending that they were all riding horses and fighting against imaginary Indians chasing them. This time, Mama was not as serene. She picked up a brown leather belt she kept hanging on the kitchen wall to discipline the boys and hastily rushed them all out of the house. She ordered Byron to take all his dirty clothes off, wash up, and put his pajamas on so he could go to bed. Byron and his friends were actually petrified when they saw Mama change her tone of voice like this, and they quickly obeyed her orders. In a panic, Byron yelled out, "Yes, Mama, I am going to bed right away."

In fact, the boys had come to know Mama well as a gentle woman, but also as a strict disciplinarian when she had to be. Often, she would not even have to say anything. They all knew that when she lowered her eyebrows and tightened her lips and wrinkled the bridge of her nose, they had better watch out. She didn't have to say a word. The boys could sense the moment when Mama was about to rage, and they might as well just do as she ordered. There were many times that Mama had to be tough. This was not at all an ordinary town. This was Barrio Antioquia, by far the toughest and most troubled neighborhood in Medellín. Barrio Antioquia was in many ways at center stage in the slowly developing war between the government and the drug cartels.

There were many other reasons why Mama had to be strong and appear strong. For several years, she had been playing the role of father and mother because my father was not around. Over the years that he was away laboring in the factories of America, the family had grown very close together. To show the kids who was in charge, she quickly ran after a couple of the kids that were walking at a slow pace. As they saw her approaching, they sprinted outside, yelling back, "Sorry, Doña Angela, we are leaving right now." As they exited, Mama locked the door, then briefly opened the small viewing window in the center of the main door to look outside and check the street to make sure that all was safe. Every night, she reminded herself that Barrio Antioquia, plagued by violence and robberies, was considered to be the most dangerous town in Medellín. This often tormented her because she knew that she could have been an easy target of any street gangster or thief with knowledge that there was not a male figure in the house. On many occasions, friends and family would tell her to be very careful at night. In complete darkness, she rapidly walked around the house and locked the door to the backyard, and then walked over to her bedroom and shut off all the lights. After changing her clothes, she finally lay down on her bed to get some rest and ponder. She was tired as well, and this was her time to be alone with her thoughts.

As she tried to fall asleep, her mind was filled with reflections and memories of my father, and she was consumed with mixed emotions that tormented her every night. During the day, she was fine. She was preoccupied with raising her two young boys as best she could on her own. But the nights were excruciating. She was filled with emotions of fear, anger, love, and uncertainty. She wondered why Papa was taking so long to return, and why he wasn't calling more often, and why he had left in the first place. "Oh, Lord, I hope that he hasn't found another woman there in America. Please, God, bring him back soon. I need him. The kids need him. Oh God, please keep him safe." As often happened, her eyes filled with tears of love for the man that she desperately missed who had left three years before to find better opportunities in America, always with the promise to return soon and provide the family with a better life. To find peace and comfort, she then proceeded to pray some more, running the rosary beads between her fingers the same way her mother, Rosa, had taught her when she was just a little girl. As all these thoughts consumed her consciousness, she drifted into a deep sleep.

"My love, books will change your life."
—Angela Fernandez

2
My first Love

"Positive thoughts will change fear in your mind and sorrow in your heart into feelings of love, and energy, and strength."
—Harold Fernandez

A few thousand miles north, now living in the capital of the world, Papa was also spending one of many sleepless nights on a borrowed mattress on the floor of a small apartment in East New York, Brooklyn. It had been a tough day at work. His boss had yelled at him multiple times for a mistake he had made earlier in the day. He had ruined a part of one of the tools because he did not understand the instructions in English. My father did not speak English. He communicated with his boss with a combination of a few words, sounds, and hand signals. In his mind, he was just grateful that he had not been fired. Although he was deeply offended by the way he was treated, with constant insults, verbal abuse, and derogatory comments, he didn't let it get to him because he needed this job desperately. My father did not mind the low salary, the poor working conditions, or the lack of benefits. He was just happy to have a job. This was why he had come to America. He was here because in Medellín he could not find a job to support his family. He had left everything behind to find employment.

Despite my father's deficiency in language, his boss was happy having him as an employee. He realized what a good deal he had. Papa worked twelve hours a day for just a few dollars an hour, without any benefits, and he was always there. He never complained, so his boss loved it. He would ask my father to do jobs for him in his own house on the weekends. My father sent most of his money home every month to support his family in Medellín.

Nights in East New York were often dangerous. In this apartment project, one could hear other families fighting, people yelling in the street, ambulance sirens, domestic abuse fights, and drunks outside. Thieves strolled around looking for an easy target. He had returned home one night to find that someone had broken into his apartment and stolen everything except the mattress. He was not surprised. This was a common occurrence in East New York. My father and his roommates were all immigrants from Medellín. They had all come to America to work and make money so that they could support their families back home. In order to prevent robbers from breaking down the door and the lock, they decided to simply leave the door unlocked.

Despite all the distractions, as he lay on the mattress staring at the ceiling, my father found a place of solitude and peace. This place was in his own mind, and in the memories of his beautiful young wife with the green eyes and the light-brown hair. He could sense her skin and feel her love and soft voice. He almost sensed that she was next to him, and he was whispering to her, "I love you, my dear. I will be coming home soon." He thought of his two young boys, Harold and Byron, with their rounded cheeks and funky personalities—Harold with the studious and serious face, and Byron with the warm, smiley, and playful face. He could see them in his mind, he could hear them running and playing and fighting with each other. He whispered to himself, "Okay, Lord, please keep my sons safe, help them become good students. Oh, Lord, please let me go be with them." My father was suffering inside more than he had ever imagined. He was tormented being away from his family for such a long time. He had never thought that this journey to America would be for more than a few months. He had never imagined that his young sons would be growing up alone without a father figure next to them. He whispered to himself, "Oh, Lord, I hope that they will someday understand why I am doing this!" He had always imagined that he would be the one teaching me how to read my first book on the green sofa.

In the darkness and solitude of his tiny East New York room, he whispered to himself, "Three years, and there is no end in sight. What can I do, my God? What can I do? I want to see them; I can't go on like this anymore." All the distractions and robberies and sirens outside his apartment every night could not steal this quiet time from him. In his mind, the days belonged to his boss, and the nights in the quiet of his room belonged to the memory of his wife and the love for his family that filled his heart. He tried to change his attention and think about more pragmatic things. He made calculations about how much longer he needed to work in New York before buying a plane ticket to return to his native land and his family. He put the cigarette down in the ashtray next to the mattress, found a pencil and paper that were close by, and wrote some numbers down. He was trying to figure out how much money he had, how much he had already saved in Medellín, and how much more he needed for his plans. But he always came to the same conclusion. With a sense of desperation, he put his hand on his forehead and put his head down and whispered in silence, "Oh God, I need more time. I need enough money to set up my own business, and enough money to pay for the house and some spending money for the first year." Every night, Papa did the same calculations. This was what kept him going. He realized that he needed more time, more work, but that he was getting ever so close. But he could not come up with a date that he could share with his wife. This made him sad. He again drifted into images of the faces of his wife and his two boys, and without noticing, his eyes were becoming watery. And then came the tears, and then lamenting and crying with a fervor that he was not comfortable with. He breathed heavily until he slowly was able to close his eyes and nearly go to sleep. He had to try, because in just a few hours he would have to get up again and start his day at the factory.

But falling asleep was never that easy in East New York, and every night he would be awakened by sirens or fights outside his room. As he tossed and turned, my father would often get up and light up more cigarettes and smoke to calm the feelings of despair, loneliness, and fear that would creep into his existence every night in the darkness and solitude of this tiny room thousands of miles away from the people he loved. But there was one memory that would easily comfort all his fears. This was the memory of his family. The love and affection that he felt for his two young boys. He would recall Byron's playful behavior and devious acts. He would recall my insightful looks and playful smile and the many embraces that we shared. But above all, he would find peace and comfort each night reliving that intense romance and love and affection that united him to his wife. Thoughts of her would quickly change the fear and sorrow in his heart into feelings of love, and energy, and strength.

One of his favorite memories of his beloved wife was their mysterious and secret wedding. His mother, my grandmother Alicia, was thrilled when she first met my mother because she simply looked beautiful. Her green eyes, light-brown hair, and fair color pleased her. The first time Grandma Alicia met her future daughter-in-law, she enthusiastically turned to her son and said, "My son, you better marry this woman because this will be a way to fix the color of your sons and daughters." My father was dark skinned, and people in the barrio referred to him as *el negro*.

In complete contrast, my mother's family forbade her from dating or speaking to my father. Grandma Rosa would tell her daughter in no uncertain terms, "My baby, you can do much better. This boy doesn't have a job, and he has a very bad temper and very bad friends." She did not want her daughter to have to suffer through the same disappointments that she had suffered with abusive relationships with all the men she had dated, men who eventually would move away and abandon the family. Men who would beat her up physically, verbally abuse her, and abandon her in the street. With deep emotion, Rosa would tell her daughter, "Listen, baby, you are beautiful, and you deserve better."

But all the advice did not work. The young couple fell in love. After dating for a few months, they decided to marry in secrecy. Mama told Papa, "I love you; I want to be with you for the rest of my life, and no one will stop me." So they made elaborate plans, and in April of 1964, filled with determination and courage and love, they carried out their audacious plan.

Alone in America, my father often drifted into the memory of the epic wedding day. On a cool morning, my mother had departed her home, pretending that she was going for her usual day of work at the local factory of Medias Crystal, which manufactured designer socks. This was where they had first met each other. No one knew of the wedding, not even my mother's brother, Hernando. That morning, one of his friends had rushed into the house and alerted him that Angela was not at work, but instead she was at the church about to get married. So he quickly got dressed and rushed to stop her, but he did not get there in time.

This should have been the happiest moment of Mama's young life. She was marrying the man of her dreams. In her mind, she had rehearsed all the details. It really seemed like the perfect wedding that she had imagined. But as she kneeled over to exchange the rings and proclaim that she would take this man to be her husband, my mother suddenly caught a glimpse of Hernando looking over the ceremony with a sense of disapproval and anger at what she was about to do. He was not supposed to be there. He had not been a part of how she planned things, and although she loved him, she had not entrusted this to him because he had also opposed their romance. She wondered, "How did he find out? What is he doing here, my God?" In that moment, my mother could not hold back her emotions, and a river of tears started rushing down her cheeks. With bewilderment, the priest looked at her, and for a moment thought about stopping the ceremony. But he continued as he noticed that the bride turned her head and appeared at peace. She closed her eyes and proceeded to accept Alberto as her husband and exchange the rings. At the conclusion, the groom and the bride looked each other in their eyes with tender love and kissed each other to the cheers of my father's family, which had accompanied the couple to the beautiful ancient cathedral in the nearby town of Guayabal. All the love and cheers were not enough to fill my mother's heart, however. Except for Hernando, none of her family was in attendance because they did not know that she was getting married.

Right after the ceremony, the newlyweds proceeded to go and get the blessing from my grandmother Rosa. My mother feared the worst. "What will she say? Oh, Lord, what will she do?" Dressed in their wedding clothes—Mama was wearing a long white dress with a veil and Papa was wearing the only suit that he had ever owned—they walked into Rosa's house. Word had already reached her about what her eldest daughter had done. Filled with anger, disappointment, and confusion, Rosa was ready to let them have it. But the young couple approached her and kneeled before her and asked for forgiveness, and my mama said, "Please, Mom, give us your blessing, we love each other." And my papa said, "I beg you, Doña Rosa, please accept me. I will make your daughter happy, and I will take care of her with all my strength forever." Rosa was quickly filled with the grace of God, and with her eyes full of tears, she leaned over and gave the young couple a blessing, a kiss, and a prayer for love, peace, and protection.

As my father lit up another cigarette in his East New York apartment, unable to fall asleep, undisturbed now by all the noise of fire trucks and ambulances outside his door, all of a sudden, the tears that had filled his eyes quickly changed into a sweet smile. He loved the sweet memories of this special occasion with his wife. He filled his mind with every minute detail of the ceremony. He recalled how at the end of the wedding ceremony, as they walked out of the cathedral, his wife looked at him with an eternal love. With a wicked smile on his face, he also recalled the comments made by bystanders as the ceremony ended and the couple, along with their guests, walked down the aisle holding hands. My father could just make out the comments from other mass attendees who would look at them and express out loud, "What a terrible mismatch this is. What does she see in this guy to marry him?"

With this thought, he would slowly drift into a peaceful state and experience a profound sense of energy and a force that would fill him with the strength to get up early in the morning to start again because he realized what a great responsibility he had. He understood that with his hard work in America, he was supporting his entire family in Medellín.

Although separated by thousands of miles, the young couple's days would end up similarly. They would remember each other, their love and their special moments and special dances and special kisses. This is what kept them united despite the years of separation and the uncertainty of when they were going to see each other again. It was these memories of the love they shared that kept them strong and committed to each other and to their family. As the streets outside of his apartment became quiet, my father reached over to the ashtray on the floor to put his cigarette out, turned over on his side, and finally went to sleep with the pleasant memories of his wife and his two young boys keeping his heart and his mind filled with love. Reliving the memories every night helped the young couple stay together, and this is how the family survived the pain and the agony of being separated.

A few weeks later, in Medellín, I had a big surprise for Mama. I had been really excited all day and couldn't wait to show her my first love. I knew how happy she would be. As I sat on the green sofa with my mama by my side, ready to start the reading lessons, I reached over and picked up one of the books that was on the small table next to the sofa, opened it to the first page, and, without her help, started to slowly pronounce the words. I did not stop. I continued reading several pages by myself. I was filled with energy and excitement that I could read alone and explore new adventures and magic. In complete bewilderment, Mama looked at me as if she was witnessing a miracle. We were both so excited. I realized how important this was for Mama. As I went from page to page, I felt more confident and I had a gigantic smile on my face. My mother, bursting with excitement and joy, looked at me, and her eyes were filled with tears when she saw that her young son was reading on his own. Despite her loneliness and her despair because her husband was not closer to returning home, she was ecstatic that her efforts over the last few years had been successful. She slowly wiped her tears away, looked me in the eyes with excitement, and repeated, "My love, books will change your life."

"You are never too old, too wacky, too wild, to pick up a book and read, to a child."

—Dr. Seuss

3
The Joy of Coming Together

"If you want to stand out in school, learn how to read well."
—Harold Fernandez

The day I stepped into the courtyard of my first school, I knew in my heart that it was a special place. The energy and enthusiasm of all the boys running around was palpable. This was not a fancy building with any distinctive architecture, advanced technology, or computers. In each classroom, the only teaching aid was a blackboard and white chalk. It was a simple one-story brick building with rundown walls and concrete floors in bad need of repair. My classroom was small, and the walls and the paint were worn, yet the ambience in the room felt warm and happy because of the decorations and posters on the walls, which were placed by my first-grade teacher, Ms. Alegria. She was a short, pretty brunette with big, round, dark eyes; big red cheeks; and long black silky hair down to her mid-back. She seemed to sparkle even when there was no light outside. She was full of energy and passion and was always ready to teach the next lesson to our overcrowded classroom full of noisy students.

Unlike many of my classmates, I was fortunate. I had a new pair of shoes and new clothes, and my stomach was at peace from the nourishment of a full breakfast in the morning. You see, many of the other students lacked even these basic necessities. Even more important for me, Ms. Alegria really took a liking to me. She loved that I was always smiling, and she would often tell me that I had a beautiful smile. She was very happy that one day during the first week of classes, she discovered something in me that she liked. She found out something about me, something my mama had been preparing me for so that I would stand out. One afternoon, during the first week of classes, at the start of the lesson, she asked us to open our books and said, "Would anyone like to read the first paragraph?" Although I was very shy, somehow, I mustered the courage to raise my hand and volunteer to read. I thought that this was not a big deal because I had already been reading books with Mama on the green sofa at home. Ms. Alegria was delighted that I could read. In our class, there were only a handful of kids who could read. I was happy that she celebrated my ability. This simple talent already set me apart from most of the other students in the class.

The lesson for that day was about the lives of different animals, and in preparation she had brought several posters with beautiful paintings of animals. As she was teaching her lesson, one of her colleagues walked in to greet her. Ms. Alegria called her into the room, and she asked me to stand up and smile. She then said to her friend, "Isn't he cute? Look at his smile, and he is able to read already." I think that she did this to motivate the other students in the class to learn how to read as well.

School days at La Paraguay were magical. We studied different subjects in one classroom with Ms. Alegria, played soccer in the courtyard during recess, and then came back to our classroom to read and hear stories that Ms. Alegria would read to us.

I remember one day clearly because on this morning it was really easy for me to smile. I had a big reason to smile, and everyone could see it. My entire body and spirit were full of happiness and energy. I just couldn't hide it. The night before, Mama had informed us that Papa was in fact coming back home from America. So that day I had the biggest smile in the entire school. My dear father whom I had not seen for nearly four years was coming home. I was just four years old when Papa had left for America. I knew him best from the photographs that he had sent from New York, from his voice over the telephone, and from the letters that he would send to us, which my mother would read on the green sofa, often ending up in tears at the end. This was the biggest day of my life. I was about to see this man that I loved with all my existence. In my mind,

I was kissing him and hugging him already.

Mama had been preparing for the last few weeks. She wanted everything to be perfect. She had gone shopping for a special dress. She had done some repairs around the house, and she had instructed me and my brother how to be on our best behavior.

I was overjoyed when at the end of the lesson, I finally heard the school bell ring. I exclaimed, "Yes, I am going home." I picked up all my books and started to rush toward the exit, but I was quickly stopped by Ms. Alegria. She reminded me to get back in the line so that we could exit the school in an orderly fashion. I came back and got in the line. I was so anxious and in such a hurry that I tried to organize my friends to quickly get in the line. We finally did it and exited the school. I made it through the main door and sprinted out into the street in a hurry to quickly get back home to my mama. Ordinarily, I would leisurely do the walk from my school to my house and stop at a few houses to briefly play with friends. But not today. I dashed to my house and burst in through the main door. Mama was in her bedroom getting ready. Byron was on the main patio playing marbles with some of his usual band of friends. I rushed into my room to also get ready.

Papa's flight was not scheduled until the late hours of the night, but Mama was ready and she ordered both of us to follow suit. I quickly showered and put on the clothes that Mama had already put aside on my bed. After anxiously waiting for a few hours, we then made our way to Olaya Herrera Airport. My father's arrival was a big event on our block. All our family and many friends were going to the airport to greet him. Although the airport was within a short walking distance, Mama rented a small bus to bring all of us and the extended family to see Papa walk out at the terminal doors after going through customs. That night, we were all dressed in our best clothes. My mama was wearing a light-green dress with a belt at her waist and high-heeled shoes. My father was arriving as a hero back to our native country. He had worked very hard in America, saved money, improved our lives, and now was returning to be with his family and friends. We all wanted him to feel welcomed at home.

We waited at the airport for a few hours that seemed like an eternity, and he finally walked through the terminal doors as all of us cheered him and greeted him with our love, hugs, and kisses. In a rush, I made my way around the adults with my brother so that we could greet him. I wasn't sure what his reaction would be. In all the commotion, we finally made it to his side, and he almost collapsed to the floor from happiness. Tears rolling down from his eyes, he embraced both of us and told us, "I love you so much. I will never leave you alone again." He reached over and pulled my mama in as well, and we all embraced tightly, crying and celebrating this happy moment. I couldn't believe it. Papa was here with us again in Medellín.

After a couple of hours at the airport, we finally made it home. Papa seemed exhausted but at the same time full of energy and ready to continue the celebration. I couldn't keep my eyes off of him. I held his hand tight and remained by his side, just listening to his words. As I looked at him, I really could not believe my eyes. He was again with us. I wanted him to know that he was the most important person in my life. He seemed bigger than life.

Immediately after arriving home, he placed his entire set of luggage on the floor across from the area of the living room, and one by one started to open all of them. We unpacked his bags, and he started to show us some toys that he had brought for us: an airplane toy, a movie machine to project movies onto the wall, and remote-controlled cars. There was so much attention. He had so many gifts for everyone. Perfumes, clothes with NY logos, T-shirts, sweaters. So much excitement as we saw all these articles directly from New York. Even small gifts, such as nail clippers or cigarette lighters, seemed magical just because they had come from New York. After he was done distributing gifts, he then proceeded to the living room and sat down on a chair as we all surrounded him to hear him tell us stories of America. You see, the gifts were special, but the stories of America were simply captivating.

The front door to the house remained open so that all the neighbors could come in and converse and welcome him and join in the celebration. He opened a bottle of *aguardiente* (fire-water) and one of whiskey from New York and turned on the stereo to play tango music from Argentina. My father had so many stories of life in America. Everything seemed so perfect and wonderful. It almost seemed as if he was describing a perfect universe. I listened in awe and shock about all the beauty of America and all its wonders. It just seemed so very different from Medellín.

That night when I went to sleep, I took a moment in my prayers to express how grateful I was that we were together again as a family, and I whispered, "Oh my Lord, please keep us together forever. Don't let my papa go away again, Lord!"

The next day, I skipped school to stay with Papa. Mama was up early and prepared a special breakfast for him, with freshly baked *arepas* (corn tortillas), *bunuelos* (fried cheese balls), *chorizos*, avocados, and chocolate. We had breakfast as a family. Everyone was at the table: Papa, Mama, me, and even Byron had found some free time away from his band of friends to have breakfast with us. He had been unusually quiet and kept staring at Papa almost as if trying to make a connection to a stranger that he did not know. We then moved to the living room to continue talking and unpacking the many toys and gifts that Papa had brought with him. We had so much catching up to do. We played all day in the house. Later in the day, Byron and I walked outside to the street to be with our friends. Several of them were waiting outside our door, just waiting to hear about what we had to say. "Harold, Byron, tell us! How is your papa, how is America?" I wanted to also share with them this big story that my father was now here with us, and all the stories from America. Yes, they all wanted to hear firsthand about the wonders of New York.

As I stepped outside my house, I felt different. I felt more confident. Now I could walk with my shoulders high, knowing that if I got into trouble, my father would be there to back me up. I even started to think that other kids would see me differently. I was excited at the idea of taking walks with Papa and having him by my side to watch me play soccer on the street so that he could give me instructions and help me get better.

As the night approached and we had some free time as a family, I asked my father to come with me to the green sofa. I held him by his hand, and we walked there together. I showed him his picture, and I said, "Papa, this is the place where I came to speak with you when you were away, and this is the place where Mama read your letters and showed us the pictures that you sent from America." My father was quickly becoming very emotional, and holding my hand tightly, he said, "I love you, my son. I will always be with you." I hugged him, and I then said,

"This is also the place where I learned how to read books, and I want to show you, Papa."

With great expectation, Papa sat next to me on the green sofa. I picked up one of the easy books, opened it, and started reading. Papa was very impressed and, filled with joy, he told me how happy he was that I could read and how important this would be in my life. I looked into his eyes and said, "Thank you, Papa, I love you."

That first night, with my father now at home, I felt so safe. I slept like a baby with no worries. I didn't mind the darkness or the open patio or noises that we would hear. My mother walked around the house so happy and feeling so secure. She even forgot to do her usual routine of checking all the doors and windows and doing her final glance into the street. All this became irrelevant because Papa was now home to protect us.

The next two years were a time of serenity and happiness that I had never experienced before. Soon after his arrival, my father started a small trucking company with a battered truck he bought. He transported barrels of fish oil, cattle, and corn from the coast into the countryside. He did not have to work as hard as he had in the past. The truck was his, and he was able to employ drivers for overnight trips, except when he had to accompany a driver on a new route to ensure that his directions were being followed, or when he wanted to ensure that his drivers were not trying to rip him off. Our family life was as perfect as can be. My parents seemed very content, enjoying each other's company as a couple, going on vacations and dances with each other and friends. Papa would be there at night to talk to us and go over our homework and watch us play soccer out on the street. We were all very content enjoying our time together as a family.

"If you want to change the world,
go home and love your family."
—Mother Teresa

4.
The Pain of Being Apart

"Some of life's obstacles may seem unfair. In the long run, they will make you stronger."
—Harold Fernandez

Things soon changed for our family. One night, after dinner, I overheard a conversation between my parents. Papa said, "My love, business is not going well. We are losing money. The truck has suffered some damage on the road near the mountains in Barranquilla, and I have not saved enough money to pay for the repairs." My mother was silent for several minutes. She already knew in her heart where this conversation was going, and she did not know what to say. He then broke the silence and said, "I am not sure what is going to happen. I don't know how long I can sustain the losses." I walked into the room. Mama was silent, and they were quietly embracing each other. They didn't say much, but I sensed that there was something terribly wrong going on.

Over the next few weeks, it became evident that our family's finances were in trouble. Papa did not have enough money to keep going. He had to do something quickly. He was forced to sell the truck to pay expenses. Fortunately, he had enough money left for his next plan. He discussed with Mama that he wanted to return to America. "I need to do this, honey, it is the only option we have. There are no jobs in Medellín right now." My mama initially appeared very upset and said, "No, Alberto, this cannot happen. You cannot leave us alone again. You cannot do this. We need to find a way to stay together." As Mama cried, Papa leaned over and embraced her tightly in his arms, and they were silent for several minutes. Mama then pushed back and looked him in the eyes and said, "Fine, I will let you go with one condition, and you have to promise that you will do it. You need to bring me to America as soon as possible to be with you, and also the kids."

She realized that we did not have any options. Papa was going to have to leave again for America. Mama understood this, but she was also very worried about the rest of the family staying in Medellín. Violence in our town was increasing, and she already knew how difficult it was for the family to be divided. In silence, she also feared that Papa would eventually fall in love with another woman in America.

Papa looked at her and nodded his head up and down in approval. "I promise, my love. I will send for you and the kids right away when I have the money." She then told him, "Fine, Alberto." My father knew she was serious because she never called him by his real name. "I will let you go, but I will give you one year to bring me to America, and then we can work together to also bring the kids to America." My father looked at her and said, "Yes, honey, I promise."

The next day, when our parents informed us that my papa would be leaving again, we wanted to die. I managed to hold back my tears, but Byron started weeping and saying that this was not fair. "Why, Papa? Why do you have to leave again? We need you here. We need you to be with us." Our parents explained why they had made this decision and told us that this was just temporary. They promised us that we would soon be reunited again.

Papa had sold the truck for enough money to pay for this second trip and obtained a visitor's visa through the American Consulate in Bogotá. I was now nine and my brother was seven. We were all very sad to see Papa leave for a second time. Mama and my grandmothers were in tears. We had no idea how long he would need to be away. Our brief time together as a family was about to end. We had experienced this pain before, and the thought of going through the separation again seemed unbearable.

I often overheard Papa and Mama arguing about the trip. She promised to support him but demanded that his first priority would be to reunite the family again. After they finalized their plans, she gave him an ultimatum. "This is not good for the boys," Mama told him before he left. "If you are not back within one year, you'll also have to bring me and the boys to New York."

The day of his departure was one of the saddest days of my life. It was a cloudy afternoon in July of 1974. We all went to the airport to wish him well. The entire family climbed onto the second-story terrace of the airport to see him walk by on the tarmac and then disappear as he entered the plane. Before he went in, he looked back and gave us one final goodbye wave. Grandmother Alicia was in tears. Deep in her heart, she knew that she would not see her only son again. She was becoming very ill and frail, and she whispered in a low voice, "I love you, my son. May God be with you and keep you safe." The sight of my grandmother crying, and my mother as well, was too much to bear, and we all embraced for the uncertainty and the pain of being separated once again.

As Papa entered the plane and made his way to his seat, he felt the weight of the world on his shoulders, and he was consumed by a deep sense of melancholy, despair, and guilt that he had failed to keep his business alive. "Why, my God? Why is this happening? Why do I have to leave my family behind?" He sat down, and on the entire fight to New York he reflected on how miserable things had become. Yes, he was sure that he could find employment in America and that he could raise enough money to send back home, but deep in his heart, he was uncertain about the future. There were so many thoughts in his head. "How long will I be away? Will I be able to help my wife come to America? How about the boys?" He had gotten so intimate with his two boys over the last two years. He thought that they were growing so fast. He asked, "Oh God, when will I be able to see them again? Please, God, keep them safe." And the one thought that really hurt the most was that he knew, deep inside, that this was the last time that he would see his mother again. With this thought, his eyes filled with tears as he heard the pilot announce that they would soon be landing in New York.

My father returned to the same job at the turnstile factory, sending most of his paycheck back to Colombia. He saved every dollar that came into his pocket by again sharing an apartment with two friends from Barrio Antioquia. This time, the apartment was a studio on 42nd Street and 10th Avenue in Manhattan. After a few months, he found himself a better-paying job in an embroidery factory on the night shift and started commuting to West New York, which is a small town in northern New Jersey.

Mama was not feeling any better. She knew how difficult life was without Papa in the house. She also had many fears and doubts about how she could manage to raise her two boys. That same night after we got home from the airport, after the rest of the family had departed, she had a long conversation with me and Byron. She said, "I know that you don't understand why Papa has left again, and I know that you must be disappointed, but I promise you that he loves you more than himself, and that in no time we will all be together again as a family." I trusted Mama, and I accepted that this was very hard for them as well. I could sense that Mama wanted to cry, but she was holding back her tears because she realized that she had to be strong for us. She ended the conversation by telling us, "I know that it is hard to believe, but I know that one day God will reunite all of us in America." This was, in fact, the first time that Mama had talked about this, and I started thinking about it. At times, I found myself perseverating about life in America, but I would then abandon those thoughts, concerned that this might not be possible.

As the darkness and the night approached, we felt consumed with sadness and also the same fears again. Mama returned to her routine of walking around the house, making sure that all the doors were locked, checking the streets outside, and then going to bed. It was so sad. Papa was gone again. We didn't know when he would be back. That first night, the three of us climbed into Mama's bed, and after crying for a while, we finally went to sleep.

The next morning, Mama seemed reenergized. She was acting as if things were normal. She was determined to work hard for her family and to make the best out of the circumstances. She prepared my lunch bag, woke me up early, and got me ready for school. Mama realized that we had no other choice, and that we had to continue with our life, even as painful as it was with Papa away. As I walked out the door, she kissed me goodbye and said, "My son, I want you to continue to work hard so you can be a great student. You need to make your father proud."

I felt like the loneliest boy on the surface of the earth that morning walking to school. I wanted to hide somewhere. I felt a sadness that filled my entire body. There was something missing. I lost my confidence again, and even walking to school was scary. I realized that Papa was away again, and we had no other means of protection. I tried hard to pretend that I was fine inside, but in reality, I was afraid now with Papa away. I even thought that other kids would make fun of me and remind me that Papa had left us again.

Over the next year, Mama worked hard to maintain order in the house. At times, she seemed excessively strict with us, as if compensating for the absence of a male figure in the house. Many of our arguments or disagreements often ended up with me running to the same green sofa to cry and implore Papa to return again. "Papa, please come back. We need you here. Don't forget about us, Papa."

Papa in fact never forgot about his family. Now on his second tour of America, Papa was a man with a clear goal in mind and a vision. He had promised his wife that he would bring her to America, and he was not going to let her down. With a great intensity and passion, he continued to labor in the embroidery factories of America. He spent every hour of free time working, either in the factory or doing odd jobs for his boss at his house. He sent most of his paycheck home to Mama and only kept a small amount for his own spending. My papa became the greatest embroidery worker in America.

At home in Medellín, we never talked about the possibility of Mama leaving us. This didn't even cross my mind until one night in the summer of 1976 when I was about to fall asleep and I overhead a telephone conversation between Mama and Papa. I heard Mama saying, "Oh, honey, I am so happy that it is all working out. I can't wait to be with you there in America." As I heard Mama saying this, I felt I couldn't breathe. I asked myself, "How can this be possible? How can Mama also be leaving us? Who will take care of us?" I had so many questions. I wanted to cry, and I wanted to yell at the same time.

I waited until I heard Mama put the phone down, and I ran from my room into her room to ask her what was going on. I opened the door to her room and said, "Mama, how can this be true?" She asked me to come over to her side. She embraced me tightly and said, "Yes, my love, Papa has saved enough money and he has made plans for me to join him in America." I quickly pushed back and said, "But, Mama, how can you leave us alone in Barrio Antioquia?" She said, "No. No, my son, you will not be alone. Your Grandma Rosa and Grandma Alicia will move here into the house with you. They will take care of you for a few months. Besides, in just a few months, we are going to bring you to America as well." With tears in my eyes, and very upset, I said, "No, Mama, you can't do this. I know you will never bring us to America." She stopped me and looked into my eyes, and she repeated, "I promise, my son, we will bring you to America as soon as possible."

I looked into my mother's eyes and I believed in her. I saw brightness and a determination that I had not seen before. We connected like never before, and I trusted that she would make it happen. With my head down so that she wouldn't see how sad I was, I said, "Fine, Mama, I trust you, but I will still miss you."

The next few weeks of waiting for my mama to depart for America were difficult. I realized that this had to happen, and I began to accept it. I was eleven years old, but Byron, who was only nine years old, could not understand why both of our parents would leave us. On many occasions, Byron would burst into tears, imploring Mama not to leave. "Don't leave, Mama, please don't leave us alone. Please ask Papa to just come back." On a brighter side, I started to look forward to the idea of spending more time with my *abuelitas* (grandmothers), Rosa and Alicia. Both of them loved us even more than they loved their own sons and daughters. And we loved them as much in return. Both of them had suffered tremendously at the hands of abusive men who never supported them, left them alone with the responsibility to raise their kids, and never contributed a single dollar for their kids. They had learned the hard way about raising kids on their own. Therefore, it was no surprise that they were both ready to rise to the challenge of raising their two grandkids.

As much as we prayed for time to stand still, the day of departure finally arrived, September 13, 1976. I thought that I was prepared to see my mama go away—until that morning when I saw her dressed up in a beautiful light floral dress, with her hair neatly prepared with curls on each side and her green eyes brighter than ever. By her side was her luggage. She looked at us and said, "Come on, boys, hurry up. We need to go to the airport." It almost seemed as if it had just been yesterday that we saw Papa go away. And now it was Mama's turn.

We followed her into the car, and we departed to the airport. As we waited at the terminal before Mama went into the passengers-only area, I remained by her side, not looking up to her eyes but staying quiet and holding my tears back. Family and friends had made the journey to the airport. Everyone seemed so happy and cordial. People would give her words of advice and congratulate her and wish her the best with warm hugs and embraces. I stayed by her side, but I was so sad that I just kept my head down. I couldn't wish her happy thoughts. I felt so guilty, but I was sad, very sad.

As we approached her entrance to the passengers' area, Mama bent down and embraced me and told me how much she loved me. "My son, I will never forget about you. I promise that very soon, you and your brother will be with us in America." I said, "Fine, Mama. I love you. Please come back soon, Mama." As she turned away, I noticed that she was also crying. In fact, my mama had cried in silence almost every day since she made the decision to leave. She didn't know what was harder, to be away from her boys or to be away from her husband. She would soon find out.

As the flight was boarding, we went up to the terrace of the airport to see Mama walk through the passageway tarmac on her way to the plane. As she walked over, we waved her kisses and goodbyes, and we prayed for her that she would be safe. As Mama walked onto the plane, I embraced my *abuelitas* tightly. Although I was very sad, I felt their love and their strength, and I was at peace that they would take excellent care of us. Together, we said a prayer and waved the plane goodbye as it slowly rode away into the clouds and then started its flight into the air toward the capital of the world, New York.

As we exited the airport, we decided to walk home in the company of other family and friends. Our house was not far from the airport. I remained quiet as we made our way, fearing the consequences of Mama's departure. So many thoughts and questions in my mind. I loved my *abuelitas*, but I knew deep inside that no person on Earth could possibly fill the void created by having both parents away, and especially Mama. She was the person that I had grown to love and depend on even more in the absence of Papa. For all my existence, Mama had been the life of the house and our lives. Now she was gone far away as well, and I had no idea when I would see her again. After the lonely walk to our house, we reached home. Grandma Rosa reached into her pocket to pull out the keys and opened the front door of our house. The four of us walked inside only to face an empty house devoid of the love and energy that Mama provided us every day. So many questions and so many fears now that things were changing rapidly in Barrio Antioquia.

About ten hours later, we received a call from New York. Great news, Mama was well. Her trip to New York had been a success, and she was already in the company of Papa in their apartment in New York. I briefly got on the phone, but upon hearing Mama's voice, I started to cry and had to give the phone back to Grandma Rosa. Grandma Alicia reached out and embraced me, telling me that "things will be fine, son, you need to be strong and patient because soon you will join your parents again. Keep praying and imagining, and it will happen." And so I did. I prayed every night so that I could see my parents again, and I kept those images in my head.

A few weeks after arriving in America, my parents moved to West New York, New Jersey, and my mama found a job making blouses at a local clothing factory just a few blocks from their apartment. They needed the extra income, and this kept her occupied so that she would not be constantly thinking about her two young boys now thousands of miles away. Each day that my parents left for work, they were fearful of not returning home, because the Immigration and Naturalization Service, more commonly known in the Hispanic community as *La Migra*, seemed to have a particular attachment to the corners and streets of their neighborhood, and my parents' factories were frequently inspected. Fortunately for them, among West New York's factories was a network of informants who would notify workers whenever an immigration officer was close by. To avoid the inspectors, the undocumented workers would leave through the back or side doors. My parents, who did not have green cards or work visas, had to sprint out of their workplaces several times. They were fearful of being suddenly separated from each other. It was not uncommon for an undocumented immigrant to be discovered, jailed, and deported before he or she could ever return home to a spouse.

In 1978, there was no glimmer of hope that the government had any plans to find a solution. As my parents continued to labor in the factories of America, and at the same time hide from the immigration agency, in Medellín we attempted to live as normally as we could. However, every day seemed an eternity without our parents, and the same was true for them. My mother had the insight that this could not go this way forever. Something had to be done.

"There are no goodbyes for us. Wherever you are, you will always be in my heart."
—Mahatma Ghandi

5.
The Wimpy Kid

"Believe it or not, your parents and grandparents will give their life for you in a second."
—Harold Fernandez

As I lay down on my bed in a deep sleep, Grandma Rosa leaned over and with a soft voice so as not to frighten me said, "Harito, baby, you must get up. It's time to get to school." I was so tired that when I opened my eyes and rubbed my hands over my eyelids, I was surprised to see my grandma by the bedside. My first impulse was to ask her, "Where is my mama?" But then I remembered the events of the previous day. My mother was gone, and she was now with my father far away in America. Quietly and with my head down, I pushed away the soft cotton blanket that I'd had since I was a few years old and made my way to the shower. As I walked down the short hall, Grandma Rosa quickly put a blanket over my bare shoulders to protect me from the cool morning air entering through the open patio. Grandma Rosa realized how sad I must have been, and she was trying her best to show me love, compassion, and understanding. My grandmas loved us so much that they would have given their lives just so that we would not be going through the pain of missing our parents.

I was now in fourth grade and Byron was in second. Byron was always a little slow to get up, so Grandma Rosa had to spend more time with him. After he'd finally get up with her help, she'd wrap up his entire body in a blanket like a newborn and help him along on his way to the shower. Otherwise, Byron would not get up.

After getting dressed, I walked over to the breakfast table to find a large cup of warm chocolate, a freshly baked *arepa*, *bunuelos*, and scrambled eggs. After breakfast, my brother and I picked up our lunch bags and walked to the front door. There, both grandmas stopped us and gave us a blessing with the sign of the cross, saying a little prayer to ask the Lord to watch over us.

Although my grandmas poured all their heart and soul into making sure that we were happy, I felt terribly lonely without my parents. Some days I felt even angry that they had both departed. I often asked myself silly questions such as, "How can they say that they love me if they left so far away?" But deep down inside, I knew that my parents loved us more than anything else in their lives. I knew that my parents would sacrifice their own lives so that we could do well.

My grandmothers were strong women. Rosa, my maternal grandmother, had three other kids: Hernando, Hector, and Nuvia. She had not been so lucky in her relationships. Many times, she had been physically and emotionally abused and found herself homeless with her children. This forced her to come and live with her own mother, Deborah, who owned the house right next door. Grandma Alicia had also been abused by her husband and settled by herself, eventually building a small *arepa* factory in the yard of her house to support herself. This was where she labored for many years, making enough money to support herself and help out the rest of the family, including my parents when my father could not find work in Medellín.

After a few weeks, my elderly grandmothers, Byron, and I settled into a comfortable daily routine. But outside the quiet and the peace of our home, the streets of Barrio Antioquia and Medellín were becoming much more dangerous. Rapidly, guns from America were replacing knives, and the level of violence was devastating.

Eating arepas every day, my cheeks were so plump and red that other kids called me the kid with the big cheeks, or *cacheton* in Spanish. But it wasn't just me. Byron also had big, red cheeks, and so he was also called *cacheton*. Some of the other kids on the block believed that this was because we had better food. They believed that because my parents were living and working in America and sent money back each month, we had better access to food, clothing, and other necessities, things that many of my friends did not have, such as shoes, milk, meat, or toilet paper. It wasn't that we were rich or that we lived in luxury, but that we actually had access to many of the basic necessities of life that many of my friends did not have. However, what my friends did not know was how sad I was every day without my parents.

Slowly, my behavior changed. I became more withdrawn from social contact, and my friendly and outgoing personality started to change. In school I was no longer the kid with the beautiful warm smile who walked around the courtyard full of confidence. Ms. Alegria was no longer my classroom teacher, but I would see her often walking around the courtyard at school. One afternoon she must have seen how sad I was, and she leaned over and asked, "Why so serious, Harold? Where is that beautiful smile?" I replied, "I am doing fine, Ms. Alegria, I am just a little sad because my parents are away in America." She opened her arms and gave me a warm embrace and said, "Harold, you must keep praying for them and trust that you will soon be together again." Trying to smile, I looked at her and said, "Thank you, Ms. Alegria, I will keep that in my heart." I did keep those feelings and thoughts in my mind. Every day I would wake up thinking that I was one day closer to reuniting with my parents.

In some ways, I appeared to be doing fine, but I was starting to feel numb. Not having my parents around to check on my daily homework and speak to the teachers, or my father to watch me play soccer, often gave me a feeling that I was just going through the motions of going to school. As the bell rang to end school, I would rush to get in line, exit the building, and then hurry home to change into play clothes so that I could go outside and play with my friends on the street. Spending time on the streets with friends became a distraction that would help me calm the pain of being away from my parents.

Slowly, my grandmothers grew more elderly, and they could not go outside to watch every move and see who I was spending time with. As the months went by, I spent more time on the streets with friends than inside my house on the green sofa reading the books that my mama had left for me to finish. The only problem was that with every passing day, the streets of Barrio Antioquia were quickly becoming more dangerous.

As the days, weeks, and months passed, with my heart consumed in melancholy, I slowly reached the realization that I would not be seeing my parents for a long time. I needed other distractions, and I had to find ways to spend my time. One of my favorite pastimes became fixing up bicycles. I became a fanatic of riding bicycles and also fixing them up myself. I became so proficient at this that I decided to build my own custom-made, professional racing bicycle.

After several months of buying parts and working diligently at my new hobby, I was able to accomplish my goal. The night when I finished the red bike, I rushed into the living room to call Grandma Rosa. "Come, Grandma, come over so I can show you my bike." Grandma Rosa slowly got up and walked over to the patio where I had been busy at work all day with my tools, and was overjoyed both by the bike and by watching the glow in my eyes, filled with delight that I had been able to build something with my own hands. "Wow, my love, this is beautiful. You are so talented working with your hands and building things. It looks beautiful. I am so proud of how hard you worked at this."

My grandma spent a lot of time speaking with me and Byron. She knew how lonely we felt and how much we missed our parents, especially Mama. That day, she had noticed that we had become very jealous, almost upset when we saw the photos that arrived in the mail from New York. Many of them were photos of our new baby brother, Marlon, who was born on May 10, 1977. He was such a beautiful baby. Everyone loved him, and my grandmothers spent hours admiring and looking over the pictures that my parents sent in the mail. But Byron and I had other thoughts. We were afraid that our mother would forget about us. Grandma Rosa realized this because I kept asking questions about the new boy with a tone that indicated some anxiety and anger that he was the preferred one now, and how lucky was he that he got to be with my mother while both Byron and I had to be so far away. Grandma Rosa sensed the frustration in my look and spent more time speaking with us and telling us that soon we would also be with our parents and with our baby brother.

Life on the streets of Barrio Antioquia was memorable in many ways. We spent our afternoons and nights playing soccer on the paved streets, as well as dodge ball, hide-and-seek, and other street games. At times, the peace of our games would be interrupted by a fistfight between the older kids. Since my papa was not around, I shied away from fights and many arguments by being one of the wimpy kids on the block. Although he was younger, Byron would sometimes step in and fight for me.

The street was our playground. However, it was also the place where we saw unimaginable and unexpected horror. This was the case on one bright, sunny, ordinary afternoon when I was sitting by the sidewalk in front of my house, looking at the older kids playing soccer. The younger kids on the block often did this to learn lessons from watching them play the game. It was a beautiful day and the game was becoming very intense with many arguments back and forth. At one point, two of the kids, Alvaro and Marlon, got into an argument about whether a play was a penalty shot or not. As they intensely argued, they started pushing each other. Alvaro was a bigger kid and could have beat up Marlon. So as they argued, Marlon jumped up and hit Alvaro with his head and started running away. As Alvaro started to chase him, other players grabbed him from behind and held him back. "Let him go, man, it is not worth it. Don't fight with that kid." The other players talked some sense into Alvaro because they knew how violent Marlon could be. In fact, at the early age of just about fifteen years old, Marlon was already a well-known *sicario* (hired assassin) with a very bad reputation. "Let him go, let him go," they yelled into Alvaro's face. After a brief struggle, Alvaro realized that they were right and calmed down. After a few minutes, another player came in as a substitute, and the game continued as usual. Although somewhat disturbed by seeing this fight just in front of my house, I continued to watch and enjoy the game.

About half an hour later, without any warning, there was a big bang and an explosion. I put my head down and covered my ears. Then I looked up, and in front of me about ten feet away Alvaro was slowly falling to the ground. He was bleeding from his abdomen. He had been shot and was trying to hold the blood coming out of his body as he slowly dropped to the ground. Other players held him up and quickly loaded him into a car that would take him to the trauma center at San Vicente de Paul. I quickly turned around and ran into my house. I followed my abuelitas' instructions: "If you ever hear a gunshot, you turn around and you come home." I quickly shut the door behind me and ran over to Grandmother

Rosa's side. I had heard this instruction from them hundreds of times. "You hear a gunshot and you run home."

About fifty yards away, Marlon slowly walked away with a shiny silver revolver in his hand. He was not making any effort to hide it. He didn't run, he just walked away to the end of the block and turned the corner. He was a known delinquent. No one attempted to interfere or even call the police. Fortunately, Alvaro did not die. He was rushed to the emergency room of the main trauma hospital in Medellín, where the doctors quickly worked on him and saved his life.

My grandmother held me tight and comforted me by saying, "You are safe now, my baby." After holding me tight for several minutes, she looked me in the eyes and said, "I know what will make you happy. Let me go over to the kitchen. I have a surprise for you and your brother." She went over to the kitchen and took out one apple that she had bought earlier. She cut that apple into wedges and gave each of us a couple of pieces and saved the rest for the other people in the family. This is what we did with an apple. Since apples were a luxury item for us, my grandmother would split it into wedges and give each person a piece.

Sadly, confrontations like this were becoming more commonplace. Life on the streets of Barrio Antioquia was rapidly deteriorating. The neighborhood had gained a reputation for violent crime and drugs. But on these same streets, I also found a refuge away from the loneliness that I felt having my parents so distant. This was the place where I made many close friends and learned many lessons. On these streets, I played soccer late into the dark hours every night. The games concluded each night when it was so dark outside that I couldn't even see the soccer ball anymore. Grandma Rosa would have to come out to the door and yell my name to get me to come inside the house. The day after Alvaro was shot, when the street was safe again, we all made our way outside. As I opened the door, Grandma Rosa said, "Be careful, baby. Please remember, run to the house if you see any fights."

A group of my friends was gathered around talking about what had happened for a few minutes, and then we decided to play another soccer game. The two best kids would pick players for their team in sequence. I was picked third by my best friend, also named Marlon. I never really cared when I was selected because I was always guaranteed to be picked as I owned the soccer ball. Because my parents sent money from America, I was one of the few kids who owned a regulation-sized soccer ball. I also had shoes, which was another advantage because many of the other kids played on the pavement without shoes. We played that night for several hours, and then after we ended the game, we wandered around the block to play other games, like riding my bike or carros de rodillos (go-carts). The streets were a playground. This was the main entertainment, just playing with other kids out on the street.

As young teenagers, our conversations changed. Some days, we would talk about some of the local girls and how pretty they appeared. But not all activities were as benign, and slowly some of the kids had begun to get involved with gang-related activities. Some of my friends had started to earn pocket money by selling papers that they got from cigarette packages, selling them to others so they could make joints. Other nights, especially around holidays, a few kids would gather together and experiment with taking small sips of hard liquor and trying to smoke cigarettes. We did these activities in corners or hideouts when the nights were dark so that others would not see us. I did not want my *abuelitas* to know that I was getting involved in these activities. I knew how hard they were working to keep us safe and away from trouble. They would have been awfully disappointed if they saw what I was doing. In reality I did these things to fit in with my friends, but in my heart I really felt like a wimpy kid.

"I know from my own education that if I had not encountered two or three individuals that spent extra time with me, I would have been in jail."

—Steve Jobs

6.
The Start of a Dream

"There isn't anything more satisfying than the power to make others feel better."
—Harold Fernandez

One night as I was playing soccer on the street, I looked over toward my house and saw a group of women gathered at the front entrance. Although it was dark outside, I could clearly recognize one of them. She was the local nurse who lived just a few blocks down the road. Everyone in the neighborhood knew who she was because at night she would go around the town making house calls and visit the people who needed help. She had been to my house on previous occasions to make house calls on my *abuelitas*. I immediately remembered that Grandma Rosa had complained earlier in the day that she was not feeling well. I had ignored her and didn't make too much from it. But as I stopped chasing after the ball, I stood still and looked with wonder and panic at the nurse standing by my house. I whispered to myself, "Oh, Lord, I hope Grandma is fine. Please, God, keep her safe." I then yelled to my friends, "I have to go, guys, my grandma is sick."

In a rush, I turned away from the game and sprinted to my house to see what was happening. I opened the front door and came inside. I slowed down as I entered the living room and walked over to Grandma Rosa's room. She was laying on the bed in severe pain. Grandma Rosa was getting older and frailer. In a soft voice, I asked, "What is wrong, Grandma? Are you fine?" She replied, "Yes, baby, I just have a lot of pain in my back, and I called the nurse for a shot."

As I sat next to Grandma on the bed, holding her hand, I could see that she was in severe pain. Grandma Rosa was very tough, and she never complained. I felt sick to my stomach at the sight of my beautiful grandma lying sick in bed, unable to move and breathing heavily. She lay motionless on the bed, bent over with pain and barely talking. The sweet smile that she always had was distant. I was scared for her. I wondered, "Oh, Lord, what will happen to us if Grandma is not able to care for us?"

The nurse made her way inside the house, walked over to the bedside, held Grandma's hand tightly, and calmly greeted my abuelita, saying, "Hello, Doña Rosa, I am sorry that you are having so much pain. I am here to make you better." She then moved over to the corner of the room, put her bag on the side table, and moved to take out her equipment. With the help of her assistant, she opened a small carry-on bag and took out some shiny silver containers. Another lady who also came with her went to the kitchen and brought over some boiling water that they used to wash some of the syringes they had. They opened a bottle of rubbing alcohol that they used to cleanse Grandma's skin.

I stepped out of the room for a few minutes as they did the work that they had to do. I waited impatiently, in despair. After a few minutes, they allowed me to return, and Grandma Rosa appeared so much more comfortable. She was smiling and making jokes. This was so powerful. In my eyes, it appeared as if life had been leaving her body and now it had returned to her with one simple shot from this syringe. I was in awe of this power. I thanked the nurses and told them, "Thank you for saving Grandma's life." One of them smiled and said, "It's fine, honey, we just gave her medication to control her pain and spasms in the muscles." I honestly didn't understand what they had done, but I was convinced this was so powerful. These nurses had restored my grandma to health with just a few simple actions. In doing so, they had brought back her smile. I was so happy. I moved over to my grandma's side and kissed her, saying, "Grandma, I love you so much. I don't know what I would do if something happened to you. I love you, Grandma." As if shaken up by a violent force, I started to wonder about how wonderful it would be to be able to help other people like this. Once I realized that Grandma Rosa was feeling better and walking, I looked at her and said, "Grandma, I am going outside to play. We are in the middle of a game." She said, "Go, baby, just be careful, please."

As I rushed out the door to join my friends playing outside, my mind was stuck thinking about what I had just witnessed, and a seed was planted in my heart. I wanted to have the same powers as this nurse. I thought that this ability to restore health and happiness to others was the coolest thing that I had ever seen, and an idea started growing in my heart that someday I could do the same for others. But now, as the streets were getting dark, I rushed back at a frantic pace to join the game and continued to play with my friends just outside my house. But now my mind was preoccupied with a dream that started with the simple act of a compassionate nurse restoring my Grandma Rosa back to health again.

A few minutes after we resumed the game, we were suddenly interrupted by a funeral procession that was slowly making its way down the road. There were four men carrying a black coffin covered with flowers, and many people all dressed in black walked alongside the grieving family. Without being told what to do, I rushed over and picked up the soccer ball, and we stopped the game immediately. We then proceeded to sit by the sidewalk to witness the procession. Other onlookers from the houses would come outside as well to pay their respects to the grieving family accompanying the departed. Across the street from my house was the local church for Barrio Antioquia. This was named Santisima Trinidad (Holy Trinity). At times, I thought that this was convenient because we didn't have to walk far to attend mass on the weekends. But there was a downside to this. Not infrequently, all the games on the street would be interrupted by funeral processions that would pass through the street and go into the main entrance of the church. The sadness of these processions had a lasting effect on me. These funerals were terribly sad moments because they were filled with tragedy and suffering. As a show of respect and reverence to the affected family, all the kids on our block would stop playing soccer and just sit by the sidewalk to witness the procession going by. The sight of the coffin was very moving, with the people in black crying and yelling, "Oh my God, why, why have you taken my son from me? Oh God, this can't be true. Why, why, why?"

On this night, the procession was for a local boy who was just sixteen and lived a few blocks away; he had become a *sicario* and was killed by a rival gang. Barrio Antioquia was not big, but it was home to about eight gangs that controlled different parts of the town, and they were very protective of their territory. Many crimes were committed by the different gangs. After the procession went by and everyone had entered the church, I slowly walked back to my house, saddened by what I had just seen. As I entered my house and greeted my grandmother, I said, "Oh, Grandma, this is so sad. That boy was only sixteen years old." Grandma Rosa noticed that I was visibly shaken by what I had seen. She sat next to me on the green sofa, put her arm around me, and said, "What is wrong, my Harito? You seem very sad." I told her about the procession, and she explained to me how this kid had been killed because he was involved in many criminal activities, and that I had to be very careful of who my friends were. I must not get involved in any of those activities because this was how all these kids would end up. "My son, all these kids will die young or end up in prison." She added, "Please use this as an opportunity to learn and concentrate on your education. Remember that it is only through books and an education that you can change your life."

As the days became dark, especially on weekends, the streets would come alive with young people dressing up and going for walks around the barrio. At the corner of my house was a bar named La Oasis. This was right on the corner, and it had metal doors that rolled up that allowed people to sit outside and inside. They played music all night and into the early hours of the morning. Music that became the music of my life. Songs like "El Preso" from Fruko y Sus Tesos, which talks about a prisoner spending his life locked up in the confines of four walls. "Rebelion" by Joe Arroyo, which describes the lives and journeys of African slaves. "Calle Luna, Calle Sol" by Hector Lavoe, which narrates the dangers of the streets in popular barrios of Latin America. There was also tango from Argentina and vallenato from the coast of Colombia. As the music played, we listened to the lyrics of the songs. These songs spoke to us. They spoke to the reality of life in Barrio Antioquia, of kids eventually following a life of crime and ending up as the main protagonist at a funeral like earlier in the day, or in prison. We also danced and practiced our moves right there on this corner. Older kids would stand on the corner, watching some of the pretty girls in the town walk by in groups with arms interlocked and displaying their beauty to the onlookers. The peace and the harmony and the music at times would be interrupted by a fight or gunshots, and then we would all run into our houses.

As the late hour approached, I started to walk home. I entered the door. Grandma Rosa was in the living room fixing some of my clothes with her sewing machine. She called me over to her side and asked me if everything was fine. "Yes, Grandma, everything is fine, thank you, and I love you." I then walked into my room and closed the door behind me. I waited for a few minutes until I heard that she was done and had gone to sleep. Now in the quiet of the night, I would reflect on my life. I missed my parents so much. Every day seemed more difficult than the last. Every night I thought about my parents. When I heard that Grandma was asleep, I rushed over to my dresser and took out a pack of cigarettes that I had stolen from Grandma Alicia and kept hidden in the bottom. I took the lighter and lit one up to start smoking. As I put the cigarette in my mouth, I coughed a couple of times. I wanted to learn how to smoke properly. Many of my friends had started already, and when I was with them, I felt out of place, and I really wanted to fit in and just be part of the group. I lay down and I smoked almost the entire cigarette, and then I put it out and hid it. I was getting better. I had felt embarrassed the last time I was with my friends and I didn't know how to smoke. As I turned around, I felt a deep sense of guilt. In silence, and with tears rolling down from my eyes, I whispered to myself, "What am I doing, God? Why am I doing this?" Although my dad and my grandmas were very heavy smokers, I still felt ashamed because they had prohibited this for me. I was just doing it to fit in, to be part of the group. In the darkness and silence of the night, I murmured to myself, "Oh, Lord, why am I doing this? Please, God, find a way to bring my parents home. Please, God." As I turned around several times, my eyes filled with tears as I thought about all the sacrifices my parents had made to provide me with a better life and with better opportunities. As my eyes slowly closed, I again whispered, "How can things get worse, Lord? When will my parents bring us to America?"

Grandma Rosa and Grandma Alicia were slowly becoming more ill, so they spent most of the day indoors. Knowing all the dangers and trouble that was slowly overwhelming the streets of their neighborhood, they had asked a couple of the older kids to keep an eye on some of my activities around the barrio. They quickly learned about my habits with friends, like drinking and smoking. My grandmothers were alarmed that they might be losing control and immediately informed my parents in America. My grandmothers realized that this was a critical time in our development, and that the only two people who could make a difference were my parents. The streets of Barrio Antioquia were changing rapidly. My grandmas had the insight that this could not go on this way forever. Something had to be done.

"Life's most persistent and urgent question is 'what are you doing for others?'"
—Martin Luther King, Jr.

7.
For Love and Family

"When everything else fails, you can trust that your parents will never give up on you."
—Harold Fernandez

One cold night in January of 1978, in the corner of their tiny kitchen, at the small, rounded dinner table, Mama and Papa discussed what to do about their young boys in Colombia. This was not unusual; this was what they had been agonizing about every night for the last year. Earlier in the day they had spoken to Grandma Rosa by phone, and she had informed them about my misbehavior, like smoking cigarettes, taking sips of hard liquor with friends, and skipping school. They had been alarmed and saddened by the news. Their discussion at the dinner table swiftly turned from the weather forecast and how to manage their budget so they could save money, into a more serious and pressing discussion about their boys thousands of miles away. They felt helpless, and as much as it hurt them deep in their hearts, they both realized that they had to discuss this. But these talks were often so painful and frustrating that they both unconsciously agreed to leave it to the end of their dinner time.

Then, suddenly, Mama's expression became very serious, and in a firm voice, she said, "Alberto, I want to bring the boys here immediately. They cannot stay in Medellín one more day. I cannot exist like this anymore. I need my sons here with us. I promise that I will work really hard so we can save some money and bring them to America." As she finished, tears of sadness gently rolled down her cheeks. Alberto leaned over to her and held her tight for a few minutes, and then answered in a calm voice, "Yes, I know, honey, but it is not that easy, and the trip can be dangerous. This is something that we really need to think about and plan carefully. We can't just decide on a moment's impulse." With a look of anger and frustration, my mama looked him straight in the eyes and said, "No, Alberto, you don't understand. We are losing our sons to the violence in Medellín. We can't wait one more day. We need to do something now. For God's sake, Harold is only twelve years old and he is starting to taste alcohol." As she was saying this, a commercial in the background on the television set came on, and she heard, "It is now 10 p.m., do you know where your kids are tonight?" Right at that moment, my mama felt as if the weight of the world was collapsing on her body, and she could not control her emotions. She started sobbing, turned away, and ran into the bedroom to cry in solitude. My father tried to stop her and console her. "Honey, wait, I love our sons also, we just have to find a safe way to bring them here." Mama rushed past him and repeated, "You don't understand. You just don't understand." This was not the first night that the young immigrant couple in America had this painful discussion about the fate of their kids. This was an agonizing conversation that often would end up as an argument along with feelings of desperation, frustration, and a sea of tears.

The next morning was even colder than the previous night. My mama made her way from her apartment on 61st Street and Palisade Avenue to the clothing factory where she worked on 62nd Street and Broadway. It had been snowing all night, and she had some difficulty walking and avoiding the slippery streets. She paced slowly and carefully to avoid a fall. She had been in America only a few years, and she still felt awkward walking on the snow. She had briefly considered skipping work because of the weather, and because of the unpleasant argument she had with my papa the night before, but decided to put up with the struggle because they had made some calculations the night before at the dinner table and they had come to the realization that they needed to save more money. A lot more money, in fact.

As my mother reached the front entrance of the factory, she quietly said a little prayer and thanked the Lord that she had made it and begged the Lord to keep her sons safe. In fact, Mama included us in every prayer she offered to the Lord. She then went inside, punched her card at the entrance, and rushed down the aisle to her sewing machine in the back of the factory. She was early, and only her boss and a fellow coworker named Josefina had arrived. She quickly greeted her friend and proceeded to sit at the sewing machine and then prepared her workspace following the same routine that she did every morning. Determined to be very productive because she was paid by the number of blouses that she completed, not by the time that she was there, she leaned over to pick up the bundle of blouses lying next to her machine. She hurried to turn the power on the machine and sat down to start her day. Then, in a sudden outburst of emotion, her eyes swelled up with tears and she could no longer contain her sentiments, and she started crying uncontrollably. All morning she had kept her emotions under control. She didn't like to cry in front of her husband because this would upset him, and this was already causing tension between them. She had done well until this moment, and then she recalled the conversation that they had the previous day with Grandma Rosa about my activities in the dangerous streets of the barrio. She understood that this was an important time for our development.

She tried to keep her crying discreet, but her friend Josefina saw her crying and quickly rushed over and asked, "What is wrong, Angelita? Why are you crying, my dear?" In fact, Josefina knew exactly why my mama was desperately crying. This was not the first time. Josefina wrapped her arms around my mama and held her as she sobbed and tried to regain her composure.

After a few moments, Josefina then said, "You don't have to cry, Angelita, I know how you can bring your sons to America. I know someone in Medellín who can make all the arrangements, and your sons can come with my daughter, Marina. It is very easy, and it only takes three days. It involves making a trip to a small island in the Bahamas, and then coming to Miami on a boat. It is safe, and many people are doing it every day. Trust me, Angela. Your sons can come and be with you, and the trip only takes three days. You don't have to suffer anymore." Mama lifted her head and looked Josefina straight in her eyes. She wanted to know more. Josefina felt a special connection with my mother. She was also an immigrant and was going through the same problems with her daughter, Marina, who was away also in Medellín; they had not seen each other for a long time. Josefina looked at Mama and said, "Listen carefully. My daughter Marina and her friend will be coming through this arrangement, and she can bring your two boys with her. It is quick and safe, and I promise that your kids will be here in three days after leaving Medellín."

This was not the first time that Mama had heard of plans to bring me and my brother to America. Many times, my parents had inquired with friends and others about the possibility of their sons getting smuggled through the Mexican border. But they had heard so many bad stories, and it seemed so difficult for a couple of young kids to accomplish this. They had also heard of organized trips through the Bahamas coming to the coast of Miami, but they had also heard of many misadventures in the dangerous strip of water separating Miami from the Bahamas. In their conversations, they always came to the same conclusion, that it was too dangerous for their sons. But today there was something special about what Josefina was promising. Mama thought that this must be safe because we would be coming with Josefina's daughter, who was a trusted adult. Mama nodded her head in approval, now regaining control of her emotions, and at that moment she felt a sense of peace inside her heart and decided that this was the right moment to make this happen. She looked over at Josefina with gratitude and said, "Thank you, Josefina. This is what I had been waiting for. I trust you, and I trust that the Lord will keep my boys safe. I will speak to my husband tonight, and I will call you later to start to get all the details." Mama had made up her mind. Nothing or no one was going to stop her. She seemed reenergized for the rest of the day. She was now able to concentrate on her work, and in her mind started to plan what she was going to tell Papa to convince him about this plan. During their brief time for lunch, Mama approached Josefina and started to get some of the details about this plan and the contacts in Medellín. She wanted to know all the details so she could tell my father at the dinner table.

That night, the couple had dinner and briefly discussed the events at work. Then Mama said, "Alberto, we need to talk." Papa quickly stopped what he was doing and looked at my mother as she started to share with him the conversation that she had with Josefina at work about bringing us to America. Papa listened with caution and carefully asked questions about some of the details. Tonight, he saw something different in his wife that he had not seen in all their previous discussions. Her eyes were glowing, her cheeks were alive, and her voice was uplifting as she described her conversation with Josefina. She concluded by saying, "I know this is risky, and I know that there is some danger, but I trust Josefina that this will be safe, and I trust God that he will bring our sons alive to America. Trust me, my love, I can feel it in my heart and in my soul." Papa leaned over to her and with a warm embrace he looked into her eyes and said, "Fine, my love, I trust you and God, and I agree to proceed with the plan. I love you." With tears of joy, the couple embraced and shared a determination to use all their energy to make this happen. Without skipping a beat, Mama rushed over to pick up the phone by the night table and informed Grandma Rosa of the decision they had reached to bring my brother and me to America. When Grandma Rosa heard the news, she said, "God bless you, my daughter, I am so happy to hear this. I know the kids will be very happy, and I will start praying so that they will be safe during the trip." Grandma Rosa realized that there was some danger with the trip but also realized that my parents did not have an option, and she had faith that the Lord would keep us safe during the trip.

After hanging up the phone, Grandma Rosa was so happy that she rushed outside the house into the street to look for me and Byron. It was already dark outside, but she knew that we would be playing soccer nearby. That was what we did every day until it was so dark outside that we could not even see the soccer ball. As she stepped out on the sidewalk, she started yelling for us. "Harold, Byron, come inside! I have great news." I heard my grandma's voice and initially tried to ignore it, but soon realized that my grandmother was still calling our names, so I quickly left the game and rushed over to Grandma Rosa. "Grandma, Grandma, are you okay? What is wrong, Grandma?" I was nervous and thought that there was something wrong, but as I got closer to her, I saw that her face was glowing with happiness and a beautiful smile. She quickly answered, "No, my son, everything is fine. I just got off the phone with your mama, and she informed me that you and your brother will be going to American in a few months." I was speechless and motionless. After a few seconds, I regained my composure and said, "Are you sure, Grandma? Are you sure?" She answered, "Yes, my son, you are going to be with your parents. We have to go and see the person who will make all the arrangements tomorrow." I could not believe what I was hearing. Byron was also there, and his face was filled with delight. We looked at each other and started running around, yelling, "We are going to see our parents." Grandma Rosa quickly ordered us to come inside the house and proceeded to tell us that we could not tell anyone that we were leaving. "You cannot tell anyone. This has to be kept a secret." This was difficult because we were so happy that we just wanted to yell it out from the top of our lungs.

The next day, we got up early and accompanied Grandma Rosa to see the man who was going to make it happen. The organizer of the trip was an older gentleman named Uriel, and he lived in El Poblado, which is the upscale section of Medellín. Grandma Alicia had been ill, so she did not come with us, but Byron, Grandma Rosa, and I sat in the living room listening to Uriel describe the trip. He looked at Grandma Rosa and assured her that this was a safe trip. He described how he had coordinated the entry of thousands of people into the United States without failure. He said several times in a stern voice, "The most important thing is that everyone in the group follows my instructions strictly." He reassured Grandma Rosa that we would be safe traveling with Marina, who had already made the trip before and was already experienced in all the details of the trip. I was very young and scared but felt energized and excited at the thought of seeing my parents again. I listened with great concentration to every single word that Uriel was saying. In his discussion, Uriel made the trip appear very simple. At times, I even wondered, "Why haven't we done this before?" Grandma Rosa, however, realized that this was not so simple. She knew that it was complicated, but she also sensed in her heart that Byron and I needed to be with our parents. She was reassured that Marina would be traveling and taking excellent care of us.

Over the next few months, we became immersed in planning all the details of the trip. We attended meetings with Uriel, Marina, and some of the other people who were making the trip. Grandma Rosa made all the arrangements to gather our documents, such as passports, permits, and plane tickets. We were asked to memorize addresses and telephone numbers. We were instructed not to share any details or dates with anyone, including friends or other family members. In short, we would travel on a plane to the island of Nassau in the Bahamas. We'd spend one day there at a hotel. The next morning, we would take a small plane to the Island of Bimini. That same day, at midnight, we would take a boat that would bring us to Miami. In Miami, we would make a call to friends of my parents and go to their home, and then that night, board a domestic commercial flight to New York to meet our parents, who would be waiting at the airport. It all sounded so simple. I memorized every detail, every phone number and name of hotel and address. It all sounded like a big adventure trip, and at the end of the trip we would see our beautiful parents waiting at the airport. That final prize made it all worth the risk. I realized that I could not be fearful or worry excessively about all the details. I just had to keep in my mind the image of my parents. This is what made me strong. I wanted to hug them. I wanted to kiss them.

"All you need is love."
—The Beatles

8.
Trapped in Bimini

"In moments of despair and uncertainty, prayer, meditation, and reflection can bring peace."
—Harold Fernandez

After several months of preparation, the day of departure finally arrived, October 13, 1978. Although I had not shared this with any of my friends, the news had leaked, and some of my close friends came over to the house to say goodbye and to share stories of our days together on the streets of the barrio. A pure sense of sadness and nostalgia filled the room at the airport's waiting area. Grandma Alicia and Grandma Rosa both came to the airport, along with other friends and family members. In the waiting area, we embraced tightly with our grandmothers, as both of them cried. Then Grandma Rosa said, "My boys, I want you to be strong and please be obedient to your parents. Help them wash the dishes, and don't fight with each other because your parents are working very hard. I love you and I will always love you and remember you. Above all, remember to work hard in school so you can make your parents proud."

This was such a difficult moment for Grandma Rosa and Grandma Alicia. In their minds they remembered the many times that they had been in this airport to say goodbye to their loved ones, first Papa, then Mama, and other family members in between. Each time with mixed emotions—glad that they were leaving for the promise and opportunity of a better life in America, but so sad that they were going far away. But there was one part of this separation that was more painful than the distance. No one could predict how long we would be away. Even more upsetting was that my grandmothers feared they would never see us again. This morning was especially hard because we had always lived with our grandmothers, since birth, and for the last two years they had been in charge of our care. We had become very close. As I embraced my Grandmother Rosa, I looked her in the eyes and gave her a kiss, and with the innocence and hope that only a child can possess, said, "I love you, Grandma, and I promise to see you again soon." Grandma Rosa smiled and hugged me again with a fervor and warmth that I will never forget. Grandma Alicia was quiet and more reserved, and she hugged both of us and simply said, "I love you more than anything in my life, and I will be praying that we see each other soon."

We then accompanied Marina and the other passengers to the passengers-only area and then through the tarmac on our way to the short walk leading to the plane. As I walked over, I looked up and saw my humble grandmothers up on this terrace. The same place where I had previously waved goodbye to my parents. Now I was on the other side. It all seemed so exciting, and at the same time so sad to be going away from my beloved grandmothers who were crying. Once inside the plane, I was crying and holding my brother tightly. We also feared that we might not see our adored grandmothers ever again. I had never felt such despair and agony in my short life.

Absorbed in the sadness of watching my grandmothers from afar through the small windows on the side of the plane, I almost forgot that this was my first trip ever on a plane. I had previously traveled to other cities in Colombia, but always on a bus. This should have been a thrilling ride, but instead my mind was fixated on the sweet and beautiful faces of my beloved grandmothers consumed with the sadness of our departure.

After leaving Medellín, the plane made a brief stop in Panama City, where we got off the plane for a couple of hours. At the airport, there was a lot of commotion because one of the members of the original group was held by the customs agents in Panama. I could just overhear the adult members of the group talk about what had occurred and whether this would compromise the trip for all the other members of the group. This began to add some sense of mystery and danger to the trip. After a few hours, we boarded another plane that made a brief stop in Jamaica, and then we arrived in the extreme heat of Nassau at night. We spent one night there and then woke up early the next day, went for a stroll around the city to pretend we were tourists, and then came back to the hotel, got our belongings, and went to the airport. The group was split into two with about six people in each, and we boarded the small planes headed for Bimini. After a forty-five-minute trip, we landed in the airport on South Bimini and then took a water taxi that brought us over to North Bimini. Here, we followed the instructions to meet our connection. Next, we would plan to take a boat to Miami at night. This would be the last part of the trip. It all appeared to be going really well. As we waited, my mind was preoccupied with thoughts of my parents and how much I longed to see them and embrace them.

The trip from South Bimini to North Bimini was on a water taxi, and a quick glance at the force of the ocean signaled to all of us that the winds were very strong, and the waves were very high. The water taxi was a large boat, and with the intense wind and waves of the sea, the ride was very rough. This was only a short trip, but it gave us all a taste of what our next, more adventurous trip on the high seas could be like.

Next, we all gathered around the center of a plaza on the small shopping center of King's Highway, pretending to be tourists and looking at some of the local shops. In reality, we were just waiting to get our instructions about the last leg of the trip. We stayed close to each other and to Marina. After a few hours of waiting, a tall black gentleman came over and spoke to a few of the adults in our group. They informed us that the sea was very rough and dangerous for a trip tonight, so we were going to have to wait until the weather conditions were much better. He also added that, for now, they would rent a couple of rooms in a local hotel, and that it was very important for us to pretend each day that we were tourists and not to discuss any details with anyone. They also warned us that other captains with boats were going to come and see us every day and offer us better deals to get across to Miami. They warned us that this could be dangerous because their captains might not be experienced, or they could bring them to another part of the Bahamas and not to Miami, or even worse, they could be policemen or Bahamian immigration officials. The group was also informed that it might take several days for the conditions to be better.

It was a lot for us to really understand, but Marina did an excellent job explaining this to us in a calm way. She told us that this was not uncommon, and that there was no reason to panic. She explained that in a few days we would be making the trip under much safer conditions. I believed her, and I was satisfied with her explanation. I realized that this was not a time to become anxious and decided to make the best out of our time in Bimini. Over the next few days, the group developed a daily routine. Each morning we would get up and get dressed and pretend to go to the beach or stroll around Bimini, pretending to enjoy the tourist sites, like the places where Hemingway had been and also the local markets.

Since we had a limited amount of money, we had to budget expenses. Much against Byron's wishes, I decided to save some money. We ate at the least expensive local restaurants at the marina where they had rice with coconut that was cooked and pre-packaged in foil paper. Byron preferred to eat at the local burger place and get French fries and burgers. I objected because that was much more expensive.

The group was also instructed not to make any calls to America directly, and that when calling Medellín to be very discreet in what we said and not to talk about America. On our second day on the island, we took a brief walk to the calling center and called our grandmothers. After Marina made the connection, I walked into the cabin and got on the phone. "Hi, Grandma Rosa, just wanted to tell you that we are doing really well, and that this place is beautiful and that we are having a great time. Please tell Mama and Papa that everything is going well." Grandma Rosa also understood that we could not speak of any details about the trip or how long we would be delayed. That night, Grandma Rosa called my mama and told her that we were well, but that we would not be arriving that night. Initially, Mama became very worried, and Grandma Rosa comforted her by telling her, "Don't worry, my daughter, they are fine. I spoke with Harold, and he told me that they are having a good time and that they will call me if anything changes." Mama was content that we were fine, but she was sad that we were not able to make the trip and that we would be waiting on that island for conditions to be better.

Far away from the hot tropical breezes and winds afflicting this small tropical island in the middle of the ocean, as we waited for the weather to improve, my parents found themselves in agony waiting for us to get home to America. The next two weeks felt like an eternity for them. Every night was agonizing, waiting by the phone to get that call from their friends in Miami that we had arrived. One day, two days, three days passed, and we did not arrive. Mama kept thinking of the assurances that she had received from Josefina. "Don't worry, Angelita, your boys will be here in three days, trust me." But three days had passed and gone, and we were on this tiny island waiting for conditions to improve. She pictured us suffering, worried, afraid and crying that we would not be able to come to America. "What could we possibly do now?" she asked herself.

My parents started worrying, looking for others to blame, and bickering with each other about having made the wrong decision. Papa could not even concentrate at work anymore. "Oh my God, what can we do? We cannot travel there. We cannot call. We cannot speak with the boys. How do we know that they are safe, God? Should we just forget and call the police?" For a brief moment, Papa contemplated just leaving and going to Bimini himself. They had also inquired about the possibility of one of their friends who had a green card traveling to Bimini, and they would pay for his travel arrangements so he could go there and help us. Each night, they sat down by the edge of the bed, staring at the gray telephone on the small bed-table, waiting for it to ring. But as the days passed, they became more desperate. In this difficult and dark time, what kept them together was their love for each other, and Mama's faith that the Lord would answer her prayers. Each night, she took out the rosary and prayed with a fervor and faith that she had not felt before. But as each night ended, she would find peace because deep in her heart she knew that we would be safe and that we would soon be reunited with them. Each night, Mama ended her prayers by kneeling down at the bedside, concentrating her gaze at the figure of Jesus on the cross hanging above the head of their bed, and in a soft voice filled with emotion and tears streaming down her eyes, she repeated, "Oh my Lord, please give me one more opportunity to see my boys again. Please, Lord, grant me this miracle."

A thousand miles away, on a tiny island in a corner of the Bermuda

Triangle, my brother and I were also praying for a miracle so we could be reunited with our dear parents. Separated by a vast ocean, we were all praying for the same miracle, to be together again as a family.

"First your parents, they give you your life, but then they try to give you their life."

—Chuck Palahniuk

9.
The Bermuda Triangle

"When you think there is no hope, it is the sweet memories of days gone by that will keep you going."
—Harold Fernandez

On the night of October 26, 1978, as the last faint rays of light were slowly leaving the island on the eastern horizon and the dense darkness of the Caribbean sky accompanied by its tropical breezes was setting in, the group was gathered near the front entrance of the hotel-house that we called our home during our stay in Bimini. We were making small talk with stories of Medellín and planning for time in New York. My brother and I were in close proximity playing soccer with some of the local boys who called this island their home. We were all doing the best we could to distract ourselves as we waited anxiously to get the news that weather conditions were better in the vast Atlantic Ocean that surrounded this tiny island.

At around this time, a tall black man approached the adults in the group, and they gathered with him to talk. After he left, Marina called me and Byron, and in a soft voice said, "Get ready, boys, we are leaving tonight at midnight. You cannot tell anyone. Just start packing up and get ready to see your parents." Both Byron and I were caught in a daze and became silent. We listened to all of her words. Our hearts were filled with joy about finally going to see our parents. Our first impulse was to jump up and down and celebrate that we would soon see them. We did not know what to say or what to ask. We were just in awe that it was finally about to happen. The trip that we had been looking forward to for so long was here. We could not believe it. Marina continued, "Make sure that you don't bring any bags or any other belongings. Just bring your passports, your money, and the clothes that you are wearing, and start getting ready because we are leaving exactly at midnight."

It was already late into the night, so there was not much time to prepare. Also, there was not really much to do. No bags to pack or other possessions to bring. Some of us tried to take a little nap, but the energy and the excitement was too much for all of us, so we just waited anxiously and kept our minds preoccupied talking about the wonders of America. Marina and a couple of others had been in America before, so they would describe the streets of Manhattan, the bridges, the tunnels, and the skyscrapers in vivid detail. Marina also loved talking about the food in America, especially her memories of the "flat breads with cheese and tomato sauce" that she said was called "pizza." It all seemed so exciting. Byron and I just stared at the adults in admiration. This distracted us from thinking about the perilous journey that was about to occur in just a few hours across the dark ocean. Although I was young, I had already taken geography courses, and I knew about the unexplained mysteries in this region of the world. We all knew that this was not just any ocean. This was a corner of the famous Bermuda Triangle, which has been described by many as the most treacherous body of water in the world. A place where the mysterious and unexplained disappearance of planes and other large ships occurred. But as these fearful thoughts slowly drifted into my mind, I would distract myself by listening to the adults describing the wonders of life in New York and, most importantly, thinking about the faces of my parents and how much I longed to be with them again.

Midnight came, and at the exact moment the clock struck the twelve-hour mark, we started to follow the instructions that we had received. We left the house in pairs, strolling slowly down the corridor, pretending we were just going for a leisurely walk. It was pitch dark outside. Four people went first, and then it was our turn. Byron and I walked outside together. Only the light of the full moon illuminated this quiet island. Since we had been there for nearly two weeks, we were very familiar with the area. We walked about one hundred yards to the entrance of the marina, at which time we met the same man who had been by the house earlier to give us the news that we were leaving. He then said something to us and pointed in the direction of the dock. We walked alongside the dock until we saw a light from flashlights at the end of the dock. Holding hands, we slowly walked toward them and followed their directions to go inside the cabin of the boat and sit there. After a couple of minutes, Marina and the other members of the group walked in. We sat there in complete silence, just staring at our surroundings and at each other. At some point, Marina reached over to me and whispered, "Everything will be fine. Keep thinking about your parents." After a few minutes, we noticed that the boat was in fact moving, and the waves and vibrations of the boat were starting to become noticeable. After about thirty minutes, the intensity and force of the movements increased and continued to gather strength as time passed, becoming stronger and more powerful.

Inside the cabin of this small boat, in silence, we all tried to remain calm. A few of the women took out their rosaries and started to pray. As the movements of the boat grew more violent, some of the adult travelers would let out a noise or a sigh of despair, which then became more frequent. Then after a sudden heavy and unexpected rise and then dive of the boat, several of us were violently thrown to the floor, and one of the female travelers started to vomit. She rushed over to the bathroom but did not make it in time. Soon after, others became sick, including me and my brother. After a few minutes, the movement of the boat became so violent that everyone in the boat was sick, and a few of the adults were crying. Everyone was praying in unison. "God our Father, hallowed be thy name, thy kingdom come..."

In my thoughts, I was imploring God for my life. I was afraid because I did not know how to swim. My parents and grandmothers had never taught me. I rarely went to a pool. I knew that if something happened to this small boat, my brother and I would have no chance to survive, and we would quickly drown. In reality, probably everyone would die if this boat capsized in the middle of this treacherous ocean. I thought that even if I knew how to swim, I would probably be killed by a shark. This was our desperate reality on this dark night as we faced the seemingly unrealistic prospect of a fight against the power of the waves and the winds of the Atlantic Ocean in a corner of the Bermuda Triangle. Never in my wildest dreams did I ever imagine that at the age of thirteen, I would be facing such a prospect.

Gazing out through a small window on the side of the cabin, I could only see desolation and darkness. The ocean and the sky were a hazy gray, and we could barely make out the reflections of the moonlight gently caressing the surface of the vast ocean. Then, suddenly and unexpectedly, I could sense the boat going up in the direction of the sky as if riding the mighty waves of the water. Each time this happened, we would all hold our breath and close our eyes, and then wait for the thunderous banging sound of the boat coming down, crashing against the water. All of us were terrified at the anticipation because in our minds we were afraid that this boat could split in the middle at any second. Then we would let out a sigh of relief after the impact and breathe again, only to wait for the next cycle.

I was preparing for the worst, not really making any plans since I didn't even know how to swim but doing the only thing that I had learned from my grandmothers to do in times of trouble, and that was to pray. I prayed to God that we would live. My mind wandered in desperation, but in my heart, I felt the love and peace of my mother, and I begged the Lord for one more second so I could hug my parents again. "Oh my Lord, give me one more second to see their faces and to feel their warmth and their love. Please, dear Lord, one more second."

In the midst of this terrifying ordeal, I also thought of my humble grandmothers and feared that I would not see them again, and I prayed to God that they would be fine and that they would not suffer if we did not live through this experience. With the fear of dying so present, I was not concerned with or even thinking about all the wonders and opportunities that my grandmothers and my parents had put in my mind about America. I was only praying so that the Lord would give me another opportunity to see my mother again. Images and memories of my time with them rapidly flashed through my mind, including the beautiful moments that I spent with Mama on the green sofa learning how to read so that I could surprise Papa on his return from America. With each second, the force of the ocean seemed to get stronger. "Oh God, please help us. Please help us so that I can see Mama again. God, please help us." A few feet away, lying on the floor as well, my little brother was crying and calling for Mama, and I could not help him. Our only goal at this frightful time was to stay alive and well. We forgot all the promises that my grandmothers and my parents had made to us about the wonders and opportunities of New York. In order to remain at peace, I thought of the faces of my parents and my grandmothers, and all the memories that I had of them.

As if in slow motion, the seconds, the minutes, and the hours ticked by, and there was no end in sight. No signs or announcements or words of relief from the two men commanding the boat. From our viewpoint, they were just barely hanging on to stay in control. This tormenting progression of events went on for close to seven hours. Even in the violence afflicting Barrio Antioquia, I had never experienced so much fear and agony in my life. I really thought that this was the end.

At last, I began to notice that the force of the clashes was decreasing, and then I and the other members of the group were finally able to crawl from the floor to the seats and remain seated there as the boat finally became more stable. I was able to again glance outside, and for the first time started to see the rays of the shiny morning light through the small windows on the side of the boat. I started to feel some relief. We all started to breathe better and to believe that we would make it to Miami.

Once the boat was on the calm and crystal-clear blue waters of the Florida coast, we all felt much better. The boat continued on a straight course for some time, and we then heard the captain yell into the cabin, "Everyone, please remain inside. Do not make any noise. You cannot come out." For some indeterminate amount of time, the boat was just cruising around, changing speed sporadically and navigating carefully, looking for a place to dock and drop us off. I suspect that the boat was just cruising on the waters alongside Miami, trying to avoid the American coast guard, and looking for an empty dock to drop us off.

Eventually they did, and they quickly secured the boat so that we could all come out. As I slowly picked up my body, I realized that I was in pain, and I slowly moved out of the seat and climbed a couple of stairs out of the cabin and into the open area of the boat, and then proceeded to step out onto the wooden dock. I waited for my brother and Marina, and the three of us together strolled away. We were empty-handed. No luggage, just the passports that we had in our pockets and a few hundred dollars that I had on the inside pocket of my passport jacket. We walked around for a few minutes until we found a telephone booth, and then made a call to the friends of my parents and informed them that we had arrived and we were safe.

We then walked some more until we found a taxi and asked the driver to bring us to our friends' house. Adam and Mary were a Colombian couple, also immigrants from Barrio Antioquia. They had resided in Miami for many years, and they had worked hard and done well enough to own their own business in the clothing industry. My parents saw them as the dream immigrants who came to America, worked hard, and now owned their own business. However, on this day of October 27, 1978, my mama and papa were just infinitely grateful that they had agreed to welcome us in their home.

When we arrived at their house, they greeted us with open arms. We took a shower, then a little nap. As we rested, they washed and dried our clothes, and bought domestic airplane tickets so we could travel to New York. That same night we boarded a flight to New York. On our way to the airport in Miami, I was thrilled that this was the last part of our long journey, but I was also afraid that something would happen at the airport. Every few minutes I would recall Uriel's words: "Remember that the trip is not over until you are with your family in their apartment. Remember that you cannot celebrate when you see your parents at the airport. Remember that immigration could be at the airport."

"Many years later, as he faced the firing squad, Colonel Aureliano Buendia was to remember that distant afternoon when his father took him to discover ice."

—Gabriel Garcia Marquez

10.
Tears of Love

"Appreciate your parents and the simple things in life, because they may not be around forever."
—Harold Fernandez

On the plane, Byron and I were overjoyed at the prospect of seeing our parents again. Sitting next to each other, we talked about America during the entire flight. We could not wait to see the bicycles that our parents had promised us. These were not just any bicycles, of course. These were American bicycles, the dream of every boy and girl growing up in Medellín. But on our way to New York, we also discussed another final instruction that we had received. This was to be the final obstacle. We had been warned in no uncertain terms that the journey was not over until we got home with our parents. They cautioned us that families had been caught inside the airport and deported back to their native countries.

Naturally, we were frightened that this could happen to us after we had been through such a treacherous journey to get to this point. So, on our flight, we prepared to hold our emotions in control and not excessively celebrate when we saw our parents. We knew that this was going to be difficult, but we were prepared to do it and confident that we could wait. As I spoke to my younger brother about how important this was, he looked at me and said, "Don't worry, Harold, I can do it. I will just hug them and kiss them and move on." This really impressed me. Byron sounded so confident that he could do this. As I stared into his dark, round eyes, I wondered how he was so confident, and I thought to myself, "Well, if my little brother can do it, I should also be able to do it." But more importantly, we were both in terror at the thought of doing something wrong at the finish line and destroying all the hard work that so many had put into making this dream reunion a reality.

The plane landed without incident, and we anxiously exited. We then walked down the corridor to meet our parents. With each second, I got more nervous. I felt that my legs were trembling, and my mind was just focused on the image of my mother's face. We walked together, side by side, holding hands, trying to look as cool and serene as possible. We glanced around in awe at this magnificent airport. It all looked so different. The people walking down the corridor appeared so tall and so strong. This foreign language coming out of the intercom seemed so intimidating. The paintings and photographs on the wall with iconic pictures of NYC were a sight to be marveled at.

As we approached the end of the corridor, we were close enough to make out and recognize the faces of the people waiting on the other side. Amongst the crowd waiting, there was something more marvelous hidden in the multitude. I looked around, shifting my eyes rapidly, until out of the corner of my eye, I could see my mother's face in a little corner as she was trying to look over the crowd in front of her. I could just make out her eyes, and as I got closer, I could clearly see that my mother was crying, her tears running down from her eyes and covering her cheeks. And then right next to her was my father, holding her and trying to console her and wiping her tears with a white handkerchief that he had gripped tightly with his right hand. As I turned my vision to him and I got closer, I could see that he was also crying and hugging my mother. I immediately felt an incredible sense of pure joy when I saw my humble parents whom I had not seen for years. But this was not what I had imagined and prepared for with my little brother over the course of our flight from Miami. We didn't expect to see our parents crying. I thought that they would be calm and collected. After all, they were the adults. They should have had complete control over their emotions.

As we approached them, we could not contain our excitement, and we started to run toward them. The tears of our love started flowing freely from our eyes as we approached them and finally started to hug them and cry with them. Right in the middle of the airport, we all started hugging and celebrating that we were together again as a family. We completely disregarded all the instructions that we had received. Nothing mattered at this point. We were finally together. Even that other little kid that we had seen in photographs so often, who was our American-born brother, was there, and we hugged him with a tight embrace. Marlon was about eighteen months old and looked surprised to see us. He was too young to understand that we were his brothers and we had just arrived from another country after a long journey where we had risked our lives traveling on a small boat through the Bermuda Triangle. He initially pushed back because he did not know who we were. For several minutes, we continued to just cry together, hug one another, and share tight embraces for the first time in such a long time. It felt so strange to be right there with both of my parents again, hugging them, kissing them, looking into their eyes and talking to them. Wow! What a crazy, exhilarating moment with the most important people in my life. We were together again in America. For several minutes, I continued to run my fingers over my mother's face, just to make sure that this moment was real and not a dream that we were having.

After we exited the airport, we got a taxi to bring us to our apartment. Byron and I walked out holding my mother's hands tightly as if trying to let her know that we would never let her go away from us again. I was on her left side, and Byron on the other side. I wanted to tell her, "Mama, no one, not even immigration, will separate us again from you and Papa."

As we rode in the back of the taxi from Newark Airport to our apartment in West New York, we got a brief taste of the wonders of America. All the sights were so incredibly amazing and overwhelming. So many bright lights. The bridges, the skyscrapers, the hanging traffic lights at the corners, and the immense multitude of cars everywhere. The streets were so different.

We then climbed out of the taxi and glanced at our building, 328 61st Street in West New York, New Jersey. The glamour started to fade as we entered the small lobby, which appeared dirty and badly kept. We then climbed the noisy wooden stairs to our apartment on the second floor and went inside. My mother proceeded to take us on a brief tour. The apartment was tiny. A bedroom that my parents shared with Marlon. Our bedroom next to the kitchen. One small bathroom. Despite its small size, it immediately felt like home. My mother had put her love and soul into making it a warm and lovely place for her two sons that she had not seen for years. Everything was neat and clean. The beds were tidy and had clean sheets. And, of course, what I had been waiting for: the American bicycles were next to the wall in the narrow hall that connected the kitchen to the living room. Yes, two of them. One for me and one for Byron. They looked simply beautiful.

As we walked over, we stopped for a few minutes to admire the shiny metal and the tires and the multiple gears that the bikes had. I really felt an incredible urge to ask Mama to let us go for a ride. Then my mother brought us over to the kitchen and showed us the refrigerator. She opened it up and told us that this was all for us, and we could open it up and get anything we wanted. As I quickly glanced inside, I was impressed at the amount of food and the big gallon of milk. But the most impressive thing that I saw at that moment—even more impressive than the bicycles, the airport, the lights, all the cars—was something much simpler. Right on the center shelf was a small basket with several green and red apples. For some reason, this caught my attention right away. I immediately recalled Grandmother Rosa, and how she would save money so that she could buy a single apple for the house, and carefully cut it into wedges that she would then distribute to multiple people on special occasions, like the day when Alvaro had been injured and my grandma felt the need for us to have a special moment of healing by sharing an apple. Then I heard my mother saying, "This is yours, and you can open up and eat anything any time."

It was getting late. Mama walked with us to our bedroom and showed us a small wooden drawer with our garments. "These two drawers are for you, and the upper two are for your brother." Then she had us change into pajamas that were on the top of each of our beds. Because the room was so small, they had bought bunk beds. I took the upper bed and Byron the lower bed. That night, Mama tucked us in the same way she had done every night while we were together in Barrio Antioquia. As we lay in bed, she covered each of us with warm blankets and kissed us goodnight, and reminded us how much she loved us, and promised us that she would never leave us again. A few minutes after she went out of the room, I whispered to Byron, "Hey, Byron, are you sleeping?" He quickly answered, "No, I cannot fall asleep. I am so happy to be here with my parents." I felt so happy also, and so safe to be in the same place with my parents. I was in a new country. Far away from my grandmothers and the country that had been my home, and yet I felt at home and safe because I was now with my beautiful parents, and I could sense their love and their immense gratitude that we were now together again.

Byron and I continued to converse about different things, but we couldn't fall asleep, and then we were hungry. I said, "Hey, Byron, you think Mama would be upset if we opened up the refrigerator and took one of them apples?" We debated for a few moments about what to do, and finally, Byron said, "Come on, Harold, let's go over and ask Mama." We both got up and tip-toed on the noisy wooden floor so as not to make too much commotion and disturb our parents on our first night together and went into their bedroom. I softly said, "Mama, are you awake, are you awake?" My mother slowly got up and walked over to us with a smile on her face. "Yes, babies, are you fine? What can I do?" I hesitantly said in a whisper, "We are fine, Mama, but we can't fall asleep, and we wanted to know if we can get an apple from the refrigerator?" Mama was startled when she heard this and was silent for a few seconds. I noticed that she was feeling sad, and her eyes filled up with tears. She leaned over and pulled us in, and with a warm embrace and all the love in her heart that she had not given us for over two years away from her, she said, "My sons, this is your house, and everything here belongs to you. You can eat as many apples as you like. Please don't ask me this ever again. This is your new home."

She then walked over with us to the kitchen, turned the light on, removed two apples from the refrigerator, and cut them the same way that Grandma Rosa did back in Colombia. She served them to us on small plates. The three of us sat around the table, enjoying the treats and conversing about some of the exciting things that we would now see in America. Mama answered all our fears and questions. She realized that although we were now physically together, there was a lot of work that we had to do to become a family once again after having been separated for such a long time. Afterwards, we went to sleep and spent our first night in America with our parents under the same roof. We both felt so safe and so comfortable to once again be together with them. As I lay on my bed that night, I could not help but to reflect on my journey over the last twenty-four hours and how mind-blowing this was. Just about twenty-four hours earlier, I had been on a small boat crossing into America in the middle of a dark night on a perilous journey where we thought we were going to die. And now I was safe, on a warm bed in my new home with both of my parents in America, ready to start my journey in the greatest country in the world. I felt so grateful, and I ended the night the same way Grandmother Rosa taught me, by praying the Lord's Prayer as I closed my eyes in a deep sleep in the safety of America.

"When you wake up in the morning, think of what a privilege it is to be alive, to think, to enjoy, to love..."
—Marcus Aurelius

11.
A New Life

"Be proud of the things that make you different. Don't allow bullying to get in your mind."

—Harold Fernandez

As I opened my eyes to welcome my first morning in America, I still could not believe that I was now living under the same roof as my parents. I was lucky because it was Saturday, and Papa didn't have to go to work. With the love and passion that only a mother can feel after being separated from her kids for years, Mama prepared the best breakfast in the history of America. It was a delicious traditional Colombian feast with *arepas* covered with butter and cheese, scrambled eggs, and traditional Colombian pastries. It tasted so good to eat my native food again after having been in Bimini for two weeks eating other foods. Mama made sure that everything was prepared well to make us feel at home.

As we all sat down at the kitchen table to have our first breakfast together as a family, Mama said, "First things first, my boys. We must give the Lord all our love and gratitude for making this reunion possible." Then, as she gained our attention, her face became more serious, and her tone of voice also changed. She looked at us and said, "Boys, it has been very difficult to bring all of us together again as a family, and therefore we must be grateful with God. We also have to take many precautions so that our family is not separated by the immigration service." She looked at me directly and said, "You cannot speak to people you don't know. You cannot answer any questions from anyone in the street, and most importantly, don't ever open the door to anyone who you do not recognize. Don't even speak to anyone knocking on the door if you do not recognize their voice." Mama appeared so serious that I did not have any problems listening to her instructions. She said, "Boys, this is the only way that we will stay together, if you follow these instructions." Mama was determined to make sure we knew how to move through the secretive labyrinth that immigrants in the undocumented community use to avoid being caught by the immigration service.

As we were finishing up, she walked with us to the kitchen sink and showed us how to take care of the kitchen and wash the dishes. Mama said, "You see, boys, in America this is like a soccer team. Everybody has a little job. In addition to school, you will learn how to wash the dishes. We will have a schedule so you can alternate on days during the week." Mama reached over the sink and grabbed the bottle of soap and a sponge and showed us the best way to wash the dishes. I had never done this in Medellín, but I was prepared because Grandmother Rosa had warned me that here in America we would be required to help out with the chores around the house. I looked at Byron and we smiled, both of us thinking that this would actually be fun. After we were done, Mama turned around and showed us how the gas stove worked and told us that we had to make sure that the buttons were completely to the "off" position to avoid a leak of gas because this may cause a fire. Then, she moved over to the window, which faced a common yard with the other apartments in the building, and she pointed to the fire stairs that attached to the side of the building. "Look, boys, those are the fire stairs that you must use in case there is a fire," she said. "You cannot open the door, and you must come down through those stairs." Wow, everything appeared so complicated. I thought that life in America was definitely not simple. She then walked us over to the front door again and warned us that we were never, ever to open this door if anyone knocked on it. "Please, boys, swear that you will never open this door to anyone. You must remain inside in silence," my mama said repeatedly. We realized how important this was, and therefore we both moved our heads accordingly.

Our first day together as a family in America was epic. We went to the park and rode our American bikes that we had been dreaming about for the last several months. It was such a pleasure to ride them on special trails instead of doing what we did in Medellín, riding our bikes out on the street. The next day was also very special. We walked over to Bergenline Avenue and picked up a bus that brought us over to New York City. We spent the entire day walking around the city and visited all the wonders that we had seen in pictures for so many years. We visited the Empire State Building, the Twin Towers, and Times Square. But the most amazing time was our visit to the Statue of Liberty. We took a ferry that brought us over to the monument and peacefully walked around the grounds of the statue, stopping at different sites to read the stories of millions of immigrants who had entered America through this island. People from all over the world had come to America to look for freedom, opportunity, and dignity. My papa stopped a few times to remind us that although we did not enter through here, "This is also your story, my sons. You have come to America to become somebody and study so you can make your dreams a reality."

I looked at my papa with intensity, and I heard his words loud and clear. He said, "Now that you are here, you have the opportunity but also the responsibility to make yourselves better people through an education." Mama looked over at us, nodding her head up and down in approval of the lesson that Papa was trying to convey. At the end of the day, we returned to our apartment. Mama asked us to go to bed early because she was planning to bring us to school early the next day. My mama was not kidding. Early in the morning, she tapped me softly on my shoulder, and I heard her say, "Come on, boys, we need to get up and go to school." I thought about asking Mama why so early, but instead I rolled out of bed and followed her instructions. As I walked into the kitchen, I glanced out the window and noticed that it was still dark outside and said, "Mama, what time is it? Isn't it too early to go to school?" She rapidly responded, "No, my love, we need to be there early because I need to register you as new students, and then I need to go to work. Just hurry up and get ready. You are going to love your new school." I responded, "Yes, Mama. Where is Papa?" She said, "Don't worry about him. He is already at work. He left about an hour ago." Byron, who always was difficult to get up, realized that my mama was on a mission and did not want to give her a hard time, so he also quickly changed.

After getting ready, we both walked over with my mama to Public School Number One. She stopped a few times to show us the streets, the traffic signals hanging from the cables, and also the crosswalk volunteers at the corners helping kids to cross the street. It all seemed so organized and perfect.

The school was located just a few blocks away, but this walk felt so difficult and scary. As we approached the building, I could hear the other kids speaking this foreign language that appeared like incomprehensible gibberish. As we got closer, Mama pointed to the building that would be our new school. It was a four-story brick building with large windows, much more imposing than our one-story school building in Barrio Antioquia. There were already many kids running around, playing games, and yelling, and some were forming a line to get into the building. We walked with Mama, holding her hand, terrified that everyone was looking at us and thinking how different we looked. We entered the building through the main entrance, went up a set of imposing stairs, and opened the doors. Mama showed us that it is polite to hold open the door for the next person because doors in America spring closed after you let go. In Spanish, Mama told a lady in the front office that she wanted to register us for school. The lady pointed to some seats in front of the main office, and the three of us just sat there waiting for someone to call us in.

As we sat there, we could see other students coming and going, and teachers rushing by to go to their classrooms. The entrance lobby was so impressive with white marble floors and painted walls and paintings on the wall. Then we suddenly heard the intercom voice come alive. It was loud and crisp. I can't tell you what was being said because I did not speak a word of English. It was all foreign. I suspect that it was announcements and perhaps the Pledge of Allegiance. After it was all done, we waited for a few minutes, and then the same lady who spoke Spanish came over to us and asked us to come in. We sat with her for several minutes, and she helped us fill out several forms and had Mama sign some documents. When we were done, she accompanied us to the next room where we met Mr. Grasso, the vice-principal. We sat down as he spoke with us using a combination of English and a few words in Spanish. He welcomed us into the school, and immediately he warned us that we would be expected to follow all the regulations of the school and not to start any fights. He also told us that we would be placed in a special class for foreign students so that we could learn the language. This was the ESL class, or English as a second language, and our teacher would be Mr. Cardenas. After filling out the documents, we spoke with Mama for a few minutes. She begged us to do well and be obedient to everything that they told us. "Please, my boys, remember that it is only through an education that you can change your life. Good luck, my boys." Filled with a sense of utmost panic, we watched Mama as she exited the building. Soon afterwards, the office lady walked us over to the fourth floor so we could meet Mr. Cardenas and his students.

The lady opened the door and told Mr. Cardenas that he had two more students. We walked over to his desk and she introduced us to him. He appeared surprised. I got a sense that he was not expecting more students in his class. As we entered the room, I felt as if everyone was looking at us because the room became suddenly quiet. Mr. Cardenas was in the middle of a lesson, so he looked around the room to find a place for us to sit. The room was completely packed with students, and there were no empty desks. There had been many immigrant students who had arrived over the last few weeks. He directed us to go and sit at a common table in the back of the room with other students who had recently made similar journeys. We quietly sat down and listened to his lecture in Spanish.

This was an ESL class where the core subjects of history, math, and social science were done in Spanish, and we had separate times to learn English during the day. Later in the day, they gave us notebooks and other materials for learning. At my table were two girls from the Dominican Republic, a few boys from Puerto Rico, a few more from Mexico and Central America, and a few from Colombia. All of us new arrivals to America. We didn't speak a word of English, so we communicated with each other in Spanish. Although the accents were different from the different countries, we could communicate and speak with each other.

During our first break in the cafeteria, other students started to ask questions, and they would look at us differently and started to make fun of our accents. As we started to play around with the other kids, we finally found two friendly faces in the large crowd. Martha and Maria lived in the same apartment complex as we did, and they were the daughters of Colombian immigrants who were close friends of my parents. They had arrived here when they were very young, so they spoke English fluently and also Spanish. We connected with them immediately and became good friends. They were pretty, so other American boys were pursuing them, and they became jealous when we tried to speak with the girls. They would call us names and make fun of us. They would yell at us things like, "Refugees." Other times, they would say to us, "Go back to your own country." At times, the name-calling escalated into arguments and sometimes into fistfights. I had been raised in the streets of Barrio Antioquia, so I was not a stranger to fistfights, and I was more than ready to partake in these activities.

As the days turned into weeks and then months, I realized that I was not progressing well with the learning of my new language. Soon, I found myself spending more and more time with kids who were less interested in learning and more interested in other activities. At first, I could keep this hidden from my parents, but it was just a matter of time before they discovered what was really going on.

"Stay away from negative people. They have a problem for every solution."

—Albert Einstein

12.
Desperate Days

"At times, I felt as if I was trapped in a prison cell, and the walls were closing in on me."
—Harold Fernandez

One hot summer night, my papa barged into our room filled with rage. Byron and I had been arguing, fighting with each other and calling each other names as we enjoyed Spanish novellas on our thirteen-inch television set mounted on the dresser of our bedroom. Filled with anger, he yelled, "You guys are wasting your time fighting with each other and watching all these crap television shows in Spanish. You will never, ever learn English this way. If you don't stop watching this, I will come in here and destroy this television." I instantly froze from seeing my father so upset, and I sat motionless as he yelled at us. My papa realized that things were not going well for us. He did not know what to do or how to help us. Our first summer together with our parents was difficult. We were physically together, but ever so slowly we were drifting further and further apart as a family. At times, my mama thought that they had waited too long to bring us here.

Because we had not made much progress learning the new language during the school year, my papa wanted us to make a change and concentrate on learning English during the summer months. With their limited budget, my parents sacrificed some of our planned trips to the Jersey beaches and instead saved some money for our summer school classes. They enrolled us in special small-group, two-hour classes just to learn the new language. Papa also added other rules around the house, prohibiting us from watching television in Spanish, especially the Spanish novellas, which we loved because we were accustomed to watching them with our grandmothers in Medellín. Most of the time in the summer, however, we were free to spend time with friends roaming the streets of West New York, as well as playing soccer on the crowded streets just as we had done in Medellín. Despite the stern warning from Papa and all their regulations, we searched around and looked for places or times when we could get into mischief. We tried to continue with the same habits that we had already picked up in Medellín.

This was the case on another hot summer day in mid-July during our first summer in America. Within our group of friends, we heard rumors that the parents of Martha and Maria were away, and several of us decided to meet at their house for some fun. Their apartment complex was immediately next to where I lived. In the early morning, after our parents had left for their jobs, Byron and I decided to join the party at their home. As I was about to knock on the door on apartment 3C, I could hear the loud music inside and kids yelling and having a good time. No one opened, so I turned the knob, pushed open the door, and came inside. "Wow! This is great!" I turned to Byron, and he smiled back at me. An American party at the place of our friends, Martha and Maria. This was so much fun, I thought. There were so many kids at this tiny apartment. We danced to the disco music from Saturday Night Fever and Grease, talked to friends, and drank alcohol in small cups. We drank the same hard liquor that I had learned to drink on the streets of Barrio Antioquia, aguardiente.

Time went by so quickly dancing and drinking all day, until it was almost time for their parents to return home. We left their apartment and walked home. I was severely incapacitated and barely able to walk. Stumbling and holding onto the walls, I made it into our apartment and went to sleep right away. An hour later, at around six o'clock, my mother came in and came into my room. As I was trying to fall back asleep, I suddenly heard Mama calling me and asking me to wake up. She knew something was wrong. She had noticed that there was vomit at the entrance of the building and by our apartment. But she did not know that this was from her son. She could not believe it when she turned me around that I was drunk and smelled like alcohol. I said, "Yes, Mama, what is it?" She was infuriated and said, "What is it? That you are drunk, and I want you to get out of bed right away and shower up." I said, "No, Mama, I am tired, please let me go to bed so I can rest."

She became even more upset. She turned around, got a belt, and forced me to get up with several strong whips of the belt on my butt and thighs. I got up and moved over, asking her for forgiveness. "Please, Mama, forgive me. I am sorry. I will not do it again." My mama made me take a shower and gave me a broom and a bucket to go and clean the entire building. "Go out and clean, and then get ready to speak with Papa. He will be so disappointed in you, Harold."

When I was done cleaning, I went home and waited in my room for Papa to come.

We had dinner, and Papa was very quiet. Afterwards he looked at me and said that he wanted to speak with me. We went over to the living room and sat next to each other. Papa looked me in the eyes and asked me, "What happened, son?" He already knew because Mama had told him, but he wanted to hear it from me. I told him all the details. Papa believed me and said, "Harold, I am happy that you have told me all you have done, and that you feel sorry. I want you to understand that this is not acceptable in this house. Your mama and me need to work during the summer months, and you and your brother will be at home alone. We need to trust you. We don't have a lot of money to afford a summer camp or pay someone to stay here with you and your brother. Please, Harold, do not do this again. We have to work to provide a roof and food on the table, and we need to trust you that you will behave here at home." I was surprised that my father did not hit me. I looked at him with a sincere focus and attention and listened to all his words, but I was also expecting that he was going to beat me up with the belt. This time he didn't, and I think this was even more effective. I really felt like crying as Papa talked with me. I felt that I was such a loser and that I was cheating my parents, who spent all day working so hard.

As the summer ended and the new academic year started, I was hopeful that things would be different. But the start of school brought new challenges and more trouble. Bad grades, missed homework assignments, and another fight in school prompted the vice-principal to request a special meeting with my parents. My father could not attend. He was afraid to even miss a few hours from his job because his boss might fire him. My mama went to the meeting alone. As we sat there with the vice-principal and his assistant who interpreted for my mother, the vice-principal said, "I am really sorry that you have to be here, Mrs. Fernández, but I only have bad news about your son. He is not doing well in school and he continues to have problems with discipline. It leaves me no alternative but to tell you that your son will be suspended from school." My mama did not speak English, but when she heard the word "suspend," her eyes welled up with tears and her heart was consumed with pain and agony. My mama was suffering. She felt terrible and helpless and said, "Oh, please, please no, sir, no suspension, please sir." In the few words that she knew, she implored the vice-principal not to suspend me, and to give me one more chance. Seeing my mama in so much pain, the vice-principal said, "Fine, Mrs. Fernández, I will give your son one more opportunity. But the next time, he will be suspended from school." As the meeting ended, I followed my mama outside the office. She hugged me, looked me straight in my eyes, and said, "My son, please, please no more fights. Concentrate on your studies. Remember, this is your only way to become better." After the sight of my mama breaking down like this and begging Mr. Grasso not to suspend me, I was extremely sad and angry at myself. I decided at this point that I would find a way to turn my life around. But how?

In my heart, I really wanted to change and work hard to make my parents proud, but it seemed that the more I tried, the more I failed to make any progress. Many pressures were mounting from all sides. Friends of my parents had recently been rounded-up by immigration and deported as they walked home from their jobs. In my mind I started to fear our simple daily walk from our apartment to school. Nearly every week, we would hear sad stories of a friend or someone in the community being caught by the immigration service and sent back to Colombia, leaving the family separated and consumed with grief and despair.

Each day, walking back home, I would fear that I would get to the apartment and discover that one of my parents had been captured by immigration. With each passing week, instead of feeling more comfortable, I was feeling more overwhelmed. All around me was negativity.

The language was difficult. The negative letters from my English teacher were piling up. "The following note is to tell you that Harold's language level is much below that of the other students." At times, I felt as if I was trapped in a prison cell, and the walls were closing in on me.

But within all the negativity, there were tiny sparks of hope that would kindle a small burning fire in my imagination. There was my first teacher in a regular classroom with all the American students, Mr. Sullivan. Standing at about six foot four inches, he had beautiful blue eyes and a trimmed beard like an English gentleman, and the most compassionate look. He realized that I was a new arrival. He realized that there would be times when I might not comprehend the language as well as the other students. Thus, he would slow down, make eye contact with me, and explain in simpler language so that I would have time to write things down or understand the lesson. From the vulnerability of my position as a new student, I felt his energy and his passion to teach, and I knew deep in my heart that he cared. I also knew that my parents cared. I knew that my grandmothers, far away in Medellín, also cared. Each day, I felt this incredible rush of energy to do something positive, something that would make my parents proud. Something that would change my life. I realized early on that my grandmothers were right. They must have told me a thousand times that my only way to make my life better was through the power of books and an education. I realized that I needed to ignore the adversity and concentrate on small tasks, especially my education. Each night I would recall my mama's advice on the green sofa. "My love, books will change your life." Each night I went to sleep praying for a miracle, or anything that would change my life.

"If you are going through hell, keep going."

—Winston Churchill

Photos

My father as an undocumented immigrant working in an embroidery factory in West New York, NJ.

My fifth-grade school photo in Medellin, Colombia. Ever since I started to read, my mama always stressed the importance of books and an education.

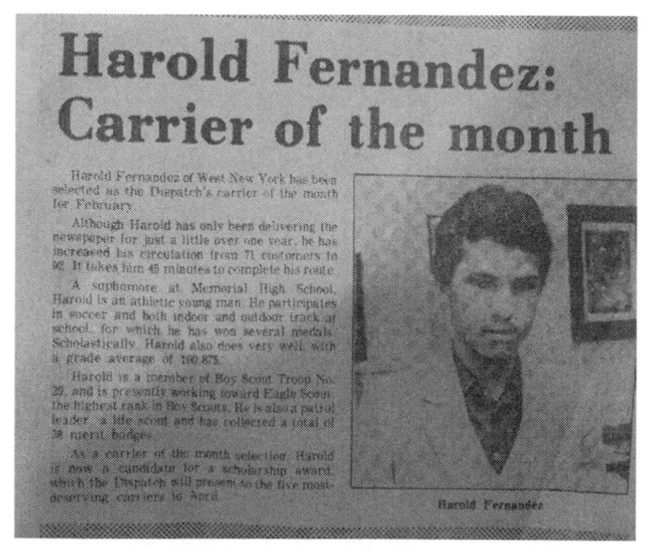

Harold Fernandez: Carrier of the month

Harold Fernandez of West New York has been selected as the Dispatch's carrier of the month for February.

Although Harold has only been delivering the newspaper for just a little over one year, he has increased his circulation from 71 customers to 92. It takes him 48 minutes to complete his route.

A sophomore at Memorial High School, Harold is an athletic young man. He participates in soccer and both indoor and outdoor track at school, for which he has won several medals. Scholastically, Harold also does very well with a grade average of 100.875.

Harold is a member of Boy Scout Troop No. 23, and is presently working toward Eagle Scout, the highest rank in Boy Scouts. He is also a patrol leader, a life scout and has collected a total of 38 merit badges.

As a carrier of the month selection, Harold is now a candidate for a scholarship award, which the Dispatch will present to the five most-deserving carriers in April.

Harold Fernandez

My first big accomplishment in America. The same energy, enthusiasm, and mindset that I used to become the newspaper carrier of the month, is what I used to succeed at Princeton, Harvard, and even now as cardiac surgeon.

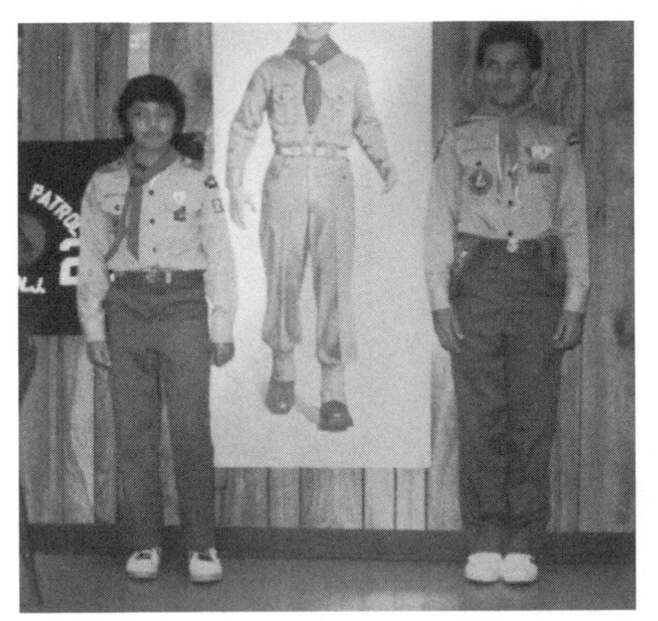

My brother and Me as boy scouts. This was an important activity that took me away from the streets, and it is where I further learned the importance of character, citizenship, and helping others. It was all there in one of my first books, the Boy Scout Handbook.

Me during one of my high school track meets running the half mile leg for the two-mile relay race. One of my favorite events.

Congratulations on attaining the rank of Eagle Scout. Your hard work and diligence have earned you this high award which is a symbol of your dedication to the principles of the Boy Scouts of America.

You have my best wishes for continued success.

Ronald Reagan

A card that I received from President Ronald Reagan after achieving the highest rank in the Scouting Program. I might have been the first undocumented Eagle scout in America.

Me as a freshman student at Princeton University waiting for the train to visit my parents. Still living in America as an undocumented student, I always feared that the immigration service would find out about me.

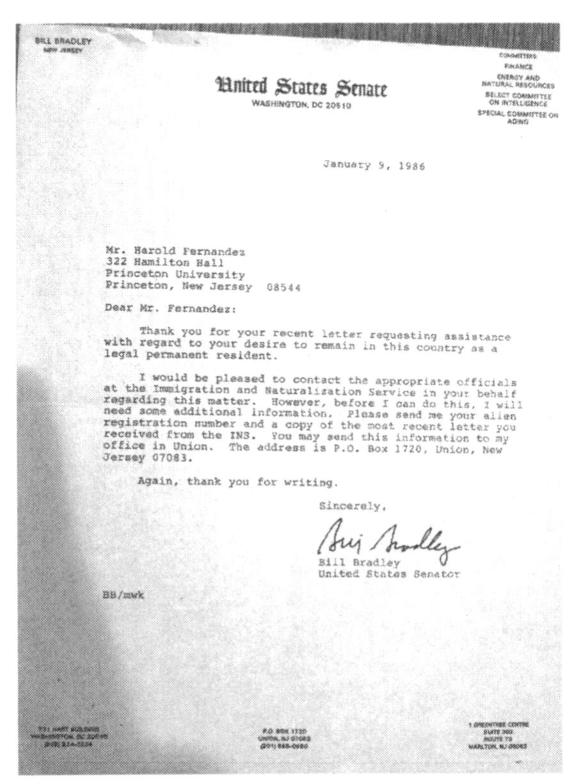

BILL BRADLEY
NEW JERSEY

United States Senate
WASHINGTON, DC 20510

COMMITTEES:
FINANCE
ENERGY AND NATURAL RESOURCES
SELECT COMMITTEE ON INTELLIGENCE
SPECIAL COMMITTEE ON AGING

January 9, 1986

Mr. Harold Fernandez
322 Hamilton Hall
Princeton University
Princeton, New Jersey 08544

Dear Mr. Fernandez:

Thank you for your recent letter requesting assistance with regard to your desire to remain in this country as a legal permanent resident.

I would be pleased to contact the appropriate officials at the Immigration and Naturalization Service in your behalf regarding this matter. However, before I can do this, I will need some additional information. Please send me your alien registration number and a copy of the most recent letter you received from the INS. You may send this information to my office in Union. The address is P.O. Box 1720, Union, New Jersey 07083.

Again, thank you for writing.

Sincerely,

Bill Bradley
Bill Bradley
United States Senator

BB/mwk

Letter of support from Democratic New Jersey Senator Bill Bradley. I also received letters from the Republican New Jersey Governor, Thomas Kean, and Republican USA President, Ronald Reagan.

Professor Arcadio Diaz-Quinones and Me. He was instrumental in discussing my case with then President of Princeton, Bill Bowen, who made the decision to pardon me and allowed me to remain as a student. This act of compassion truly changed my life and allowed me to continue with my dream to help others through medicine. Thank you, Professor Diaz and Professor Bowen (17th president of Princeton University).

President Shapiro presented the Pyne Prize to co-winners Hagedorn and Fernandez. (Photo by Robert P. Matthews)

Alumni day ceremony at Jadwin Gym where I was the co-recipient of the highest general distinction given to an undergraduate at Princeton, The Moses Taylor Pyne Honor Prize.

Harold Fernandez, M.D., Hailed as Hispanic Super Hero by Discovery en Espanol

The amazing immigration story of Harold Fernandez, M.D., a cardiac surgeon at St. Francis Hospital, has captured nationwide media attention not only on networks such as CNN and Univision, but also Discovery en Espanol. The channel was so impressed by the doctor's story of being smuggled from Columbia as a boy to becoming a Harvard-educated M.D., it chose him as the model for one of four cartoon super heroes to provide inspiration for young people during Hispanic Heritage Month.

My story selected by the Discovery Channel to celebrate the culture and traditions of our community during Hispanic Heritage month.

My family: Brandon, Sandra, Jasmine and Me during one of our vacations at our favorite place, Disney World.

My brothers Alex and Marlon, my mother, my father, Me, and my brother Byron celebrating the golden anniversary of the two people who made it all possible. Thank you, Mama and Papa.

Me and my son, accompanied by the Honorable Supreme Court Justice Sonia Sotomayor. I was not the first Hispanic student to win the Pyne prize at Princeton. That distinction is held by Justice Sotomayor when she was awarded this prize on her graduation day.

Patricia Shih (artist and human rights activist, and also the director of a documentary based on my life), Ms. Zoe Krief, Me, Dr. Eve Krief (pediatrician and civil rights activist), Ms. Sharon Golden, and Senator Jim Gaughran. This was a local protest demanding justice and humane treatment for the children separated from their families at the southern border. I could have been one of these kids. Peaceful protests are part of American life. They were important in the civil rights movement in the 1960s and they are now an important part of our society as we demand justice for acts of police brutality, condemn racism, and support the general acceptance that the lives of African-Americans are as important as the lives of everyone else (Black Lives Matter).

13.
Magic where you Least Expect it

"Find a book that speaks to you."
—Harold Fernandez

The gymnasium at the local high school in Secaucus, New Jersey, was bustling with hundreds of Boy Scouts, all dressed in their stately uniforms that consisted of their special shirts and sashes, several badges, handkerchiefs, belts, and emblems representing their rank and troop affiliation. We were there not for a special celebration, but for the First Aid Jamboree, a regional competition on first aid skills. Each troop of scouts was positioned in a different place along the floor, waiting for the examiners to come by and test their ability to handle different emergency first aid techniques. The examiners were making their rounds and stopping at each station to test the troops on their ability to treat a wide variety of emergencies. At each stop, the examiner would describe an injury, ranging from a snake bite to a broken bone or a drowning, or even possibly a cardiac arrest. The group of scouts would then show their expertise in treating that particular injury. As the examiners were making their rounds, my troop, Boy Scout Troop 129, was in a rush to get ready to show everything that we had learned from our Scoutmaster, Mr. William Harris.

Our troop was very different from the others because we were mostly made up of immigrant kids. I think that this is what made us unique, and as a result, it made us even stronger. We were very motivated to show that we could compete. In our group, we had Hector and George

Moya, who were sons of hard-working Cuban immigrants. We also had the Arroyo brothers from Puerto Rico and Hildebrando from the Dominican Republic, as well as other kids from other Latin American countries. And finally, the Fernandez brothers from Medellín, Colombia. As the examiners were approaching, our troop was in a huddle reviewing all the first aid information in the Boy Scout Handbook. After some great performances the previous years, we had become one of the top troops in the state of New Jersey. My brother Byron was busy practicing knots, in case one of the examiners asked about them and how to tie certain bandages or ropes. Every scout had a role. We were a fine-tuned working machine of young kids who had perfected tasks by becoming experts at reading the Boy Scout Handbook. Although I was also very good at handling different emergencies, on this particular night, I was assigned a different role. Part of the overall competition was a written test that was given to one of the scouts selected by each troop. Although I had a very heavy accent, I had become an expert at first aid by reading the Boy Scout Handbook with fervor that scared even my parents. I had memorized every single treatment for any condition mentioned in the handbook. So, it was no surprise that Mr. Harris and the other junior leaders of the troop elected me to be the one in our troop to take the written test. They knew that I had mastered this information.

In the midst of all the noise in the gymnasium, they called for each troop to send their representative scout to partake in the written test. With a slight tremor in my hands, I grabbed my pencil and pen, and walked over toward my assigned room. We all sat at different tables with a booklet, and after a few minutes of instructions, I started taking the test. As I read the questions, I realized that all the information was coming from the Boy Scout Handbook, which I knew as well as I knew my own name. Yes, for the last few months, since I had become a scout, I had fallen in love with this book. With every single chapter. I memorized all its contents, including the Scout Oath and the Law. I knew by memory all the different ranks and had images in my head of all the badges associated with each rank. As I glanced at the questions, I realized that, although I did not speak English too well, I knew all the answers. Yes, this was information that I had read, not just once but multiple times each night as I leafed through the pages during my spare time. Often, when I felt that I didn't belong here and was lacking confidence, this book took me from my early troubles in school and the streets of West New York into a world of service, helping others and improving myself. After quickly reviewing all the questions in the booklet, I came back to the first one and started writing the answer. One by one, I moved through the test until I had answered the last question. After looking over the booklet to make sure I had not missed anything, I got up, and with an overflowing confidence that made me appear as if I was walking on clouds, I made my way to the Scoutmaster proctoring the exam and gave him the booklet. Then I walked over to the gymnasium floor to help out with the practical part of the exam, which was taking place on the main floor. Upon returning to the gymnasium floor to assist in the practical part of the exam, I found my troop had completed the exercise already and they were just waiting for the results. Our troop was feeling confident, but we were very nervous during this waiting period. A few minutes later, one of the scout organizers walked over to the microphone and proceeded to share the results, announcing the top ten troops starting with number ten. As the troops were announced, we all grew more anxious by the second. I had already been having doubts in my head, knowing that the written test was a big component of the overall rank. "Oh my God, how did I do? Did I disappoint my fellow scouts? Did I really understand the questions?" I asked myself in my head as the announcements proceeded. Finally, the announcer called the number one troop for the First Aid Jamboree, "and the number one troop is Troop 129." We all screamed and jumped up and down in a state of accomplishment and happiness that I had not yet felt here in America. We all celebrated–we had worked so hard with our Scoutmaster and our junior leaders over the last few months.

My Boy Scout troop was really something special. We met on Friday nights at the American Veterans Hall on 57th Street and Boulevard East, with a captivating view of the nighttime Manhattan skyline. Mr. Harris was a tall, strong man who had fought in the Vietnam War, and he ran our troop like a real-life army unit. He was a strict disciplinarian and, at the same time, a gentle and sensitive leader who was always available to listen to our problems and offer advice. He often brought along some of his veteran friends to give us instructions in drills, camping, hiking, and emergency preparedness. I often thought that Mr. Harris believed that the war was not really over, and that he was training a group of young soldiers to survive in battle.

In addition to our weekly meetings, we went on weekend camping trips once a month. I enjoyed the long nights by the fire, singing Scout songs and telling stories past midnight, like the tale of "Indian Joe," an ancient Scoutmaster whose son had disappeared in the wilderness and whose ghost would still materialize at night, searching for the lost boy. Several times, we camped out during the winter. This was especially rough for my brother and me because our sleeping bags were the cheapest available at the local camping store—all that my parents could afford—and the cold would seep through the thin fabrics. We didn't have clothing made of high-tech fabrics to keep out the cold. We had to wear our own everyday winter coats and sweaters.

Our weekly Friday meetings would start with us reciting, in unison, the Scout Oath and Scout Law. Then we would split into four patrols, each with about five or six Scouts and a patrol leader, to practice our Scout skills, like tying knots and first aid. Reading the *Scout Handbook*, I would envision the steps needed for a particular knot and repeat in my mind, "The square knot—right over left and left over right." I might have practiced tying that knot hundreds of times for hours, soon becoming one of the speediest knot-tiers in my troop. The fastest was actually Byron, who represented our troop at the regional competitions. Now, knot-tying is a big part of both of our lives—for me in suturing and other fine surgical procedures and for him, in fastening together the scaffolds that allow workers to climb the walls of tall buildings.

Over the next few years, the handbook became an intimate part of my life. I read every single chapter several times, and I put into practice many of the things I read in the book. I realized, for example, that my parents did not have the money to buy me an expensive backpack. Therefore, I read in detail the chapter on making your own backpack, and I did it myself. Since Mama was a very good at sewing, I bought all the materials and followed every step to eventually create my own backpack that I used for many of our camping trips. Although I had come to America on a boat, I did not know how to swim. I still remember feeling so helpless on that night when we came on the boat across the ocean thinking about how I did not know how to swim. As a result, I became determined that I would learn by reading the handbook, so I memorized all the steps and practiced all the maneuvers in my head, putting all the images about swimming in my mind, even though I wasn't actually in the water. But the funny thing is that when I was in the water, it became much easier. In fact, on our first one-week summer camp at Rockhill in Pennsylvania, I was able to quickly learn. The camp started on a Sunday, and by the following Thursday, I had completed an activity on the lake called the Mile Swim, and the next day I passed my test to get the Swimming Merit Badge.

When my life as a young teenager in America appeared as if it was not going anywhere, then came a book. In the place where I least expected it, I found a book that I could not put down. Each night, I loved lying down on my bed, silently flipping through the pages of the Boy Scout Handbook. Of course, this is not what many would consider a great work of literature. But to me, at that stage in my life, it was. I could escape from the hassle and rumble of a busy life full of distractions in West New York and into the peace and quiet of nature, a life of service, character building, and service to others. I would imagine myself as one of the scouts depicted by the paintings of Norman Rockwell. These were not the great inspiring words of Shakespeare or Walt Whitman or Gabriel Garcia Marquez, but these were words, ideas, and concepts that grabbed my attention each night as I imagined myself doing everything depicted in that simple book. I read the book so much that I embarked on a crazy path to get my hands on every possible merit badge. Within a few years, I climbed through all the different ranks until I caught up with some of the older scouts and I made it to the final rank of Eagle Scout. My success in the scouting program was not related to me being more intelligent than the other scouts. It was simply related to the power and magic of a simple handbook that grabbed my imagination and encouraged me to realize that Mama was right when she had told me on the green sofa, "My love, books will change your life." This was the proof I needed. The Boy Scout Handbook was changing my life.

On the memorable evening of May 27, 1983, I graduated as an Eagle Scout in a special ceremony at the same place where we had our weekly meetings. I was proud to join in the celebration with the three young men who had led my troop for several years: Jorge Moya; Hector Moya; and Bill Harris, the son of the Scoutmaster. As I was up on stage receiving my award, I could not help but think of my dear friend William, who was not there with us but should have been. He had been there with us from the start, when I first felt that rush of excitement as Troop 129 marched down Bergenline Avenue carrying its colorful flags on our first Memorial Day celebration. But something terrible happened along the way.

On an ordinary December night in 1980, William, my brother, and I were walking home after our weekly Scout meeting as we usually did, heading from Boulevard East, up 57th Street, toward Bergenline Avenue in the center of town. When we got to Hudson Avenue, we would stop and talk for a few minutes and then go our separate ways. On this particular night, we talked for over an hour. William had just started his freshman year at Memorial High. With his bright, dark, hopeful eyes framed by his curly dark hair, he told us vividly about his plans for that year. As the time arrived for us to say goodbye, William wanted to keep talking, probably not wanting to go home to an empty house. His mother was not home, as she was at her second job, so he invited us to come over for a sleepover. We would have been glad to go, but our father had given us strict orders to return home after the meeting and we waved William farewell.

At four in the morning, my mother woke us. "Where is William?" she wanted to know. William's mother could not find him. After working late, William's mother had arrived home to see the two-story house consumed by flames, my mother told us. We told her we did not know where William was, dreading what that meant. There was no answer to William's whereabouts for another two hours because the fire had been so intense that it was difficult to search. When the building had cooled down and the smoke diminished, the firemen found William's body in his bedroom closet. He probably had been awakened by the smoke and sought an escape route and could only make it to a closet. I was deeply, deeply shaken. I don't think I had ever felt so much pain. My brother and I cried for days. I felt a sense of profound emptiness that this calamity could happen to someone so young and so beautiful. We looked at him as our American brother. For years, I felt guilty that Byron and I had not slept over at William's house that night. Perhaps one of us could have detected the fire early enough to make an escape. He was a great friend and would have surely been with us at that final ceremony, graduating as another Eagle Scout from Troop 129. This was a very sad time for me. My dear friend was physically gone, but his spirit of adventure, compassion for others, and zest for life was passed on to me and my brother forever.

"The greatest glory in living lies not in never falling, but in rising every time we fall."

—Nelson Mandela

14.
Only one Way Out

"No excuses. You need to find a way to be alone with your books."
—Harold Fernandez

Each night as I went to bed, I was haunted by the images of my mama breaking down as the vice-principal warned that I was going to be suspended from school. With the passing of time, it became clearer to me that I only had one way out. And yes, my mama was right when she whispered those words to me as I was learning how to read: "My boy, books will change your life." What she really meant was that my only way to change my life would be through an education. The more that I repeated these words to myself, the more I became enchanted with books, reading, and learning. But the truth is that it was not always convenient to study in my home. In our narrow bedroom, Byron and I shared one desk. When my mother was cooking in the kitchen or cleaning up after Marlon, the noise would echo into our bedroom. Our room faced an apartment about ten feet away, and we could clearly see and hear everything going on in that home. Our window shades were kept drawn, but I could hear the music blasting outside my window—not Vivaldi or Beethoven, but salsa, merengue, and tango songs of the common folks that I had heard streaming from the Oasis bar in Barrio Antioquia. All day I could hear neighbors quarrelling. I needed to find a way to be alone with my books.

Many nights, before falling asleep, I would fantasize about ways to make our apartment physically larger to have a place where I could study without so many distractions. I imagined dividing our bedroom into two stories, almost like having a small crawlspace close to the ceiling where I could just climb in and read without ever having to come out. When I asked my father about the practicality of that, he gave it some thought but said the landlord would never allow us to do it. I really think that he started to wonder if I was going a little crazy.

To evade the commotion, I would often study when everyone else had gone to sleep. To avoid distracting Byron, I would move all my things to our kitchen. Here at the small, round table in the corner of our tiny kitchen, I was surrounded only by the silence of the night. Looking outside the window that faced the next apartment building just a few feet away, I could only see darkness. It was late in the night, and, finally, everyone in our building and the one next to us was sleeping. There was no music blasting from any of the surrounding apartments. There were no arguments to be heard, just the silence of the night, and yes, the mice and the roaches in our kitchen. But in my apartment building, this was the best time to study.

These were not ordinary mice, by the way; they were educated mice that had learned the art of survival in the overcrowded apartment complex where I lived. They would come out from hiding in the night and roam around the floor of the kitchen, searching for leftover food. At times, they would not come out because there was someone in the kitchen or because we would keep the lights on to keep them away. However, I think that they had now realized that when I was in the kitchen, I would not disturb them. It was not worth it. This was a battle that I could not win. I just had to ignore them. Sometimes, they would come into the kitchen and make eye contact with me. Upon realizing that it was me sitting by the table concentrating on my textbooks, they would go about their business.

My mother was tormented by the sound of the mice scurrying up the walls and the roaches sidling along the floor. She kept our own apartment sparkling clean. We told her many times, "Mama, we cannot win this battle; they are everywhere."

I could not let the mice and roaches distract me; I had to study for my classes, and I discovered that in my apartment complex the quietest time was after people went to bed. I created my own zone of solitude to contemplate and concentrate on my books. My mama definitely thought that I was losing my mind. After being one of the most social and friendly kids around, I was rapidly changing. When their friends would come to visit or there were people in the kitchen, I would quietly go inside my tiny bedroom. I was determined that I would use all of my energy on my books. I no longer had time for outside influences and even shrugged off romances with pretty girls who had shown interest in my friendship. I did not need my parents to tell me to work hard. Indeed, my mother would often feel pity for me and implore me to stop working and take a break. Knocking on the door to my bedroom, she would call in a low, sweet voice, "My love, please come out and have something to eat." Sometimes I would say, "No, I don't want anything," or I would just ignore her. A few minutes later, she would then say, "Can I bring you a cup of coffee?"

At other times, she would ask me to come out of the room to speak with friends that were visiting or watch an engaging movie. I would refuse, sometimes rudely. I was too preoccupied with my work. I found an escape in my books. I could immerse myself in a particular subject and discover that I would become more passionate about it the more that I learned. In my small room in our small apartment, with the mice going by, I could escape inside the books I was reading and find tremendous pleasure figuring out ideas and concepts. I was also driven because I had been assured by all the important people in my life—my grandmothers and my parents—that hard work in school would lead to a better life. Perhaps it would also enable me to help my struggling parents and my grandmothers. This thought added a level of urgency to what I was doing. Given our precarious situation in America as undocumented immigrants, I also dreamed that somehow, in some way I could not foresee, my achievements would help us become legal residents.

After a few years, I was beginning to feel more comfortable with English. I appreciated that other students no longer referred to me as a "refugee." I still had a long way to go until I could read, speak, and write with a sense of mastery, though. I was especially conscious of my heavy accent. Each time that I spoke in public, I worried that I was not being understood.

Memorial High was not an ordinary high school. Many of the kids were sons and daughters of recent immigrants. It was a teeming place in the heart of West New York with over four hundred students in every grade. Each of us heard many times from our parents that the only way to get ahead in life was with an education. So Memorial was a school that seemed to bustle with immigrant striving, hunger, and determination. There was no shortage of talented students and athletes. Memorial's baseball team was often ranked as one of the best in the country, and its soccer, football, and track and field programs were also highly regarded.

Early in high school, I adopted an unconventional method of studying. The impetus probably came from the Boy Scouts and its motto of "Be Prepared." I decided that in each subject I would actually try to teach myself the material before it was presented in class. I was not always successful in grasping the lesson, but I was familiar with the concepts before the teacher introduced them. This method also kept me one or two lessons ahead of the class. When the teacher talked about slopes in algebra, I had already learned about them. I did so well in Introductory Algebra that the math department allowed me to take both Geometry and Advanced Algebra during tenth grade, so that I could catch up to the other students in the college prep group. Sometimes I felt as if I were cheating because I could easily grasp the ideas being taught in class. I knew, though, that I could display mastery of the day's material not because I was smarter than the other kids, but because I had already learned it on my own.

My hard work was being noticed by the school. One afternoon, after the end of the first marking-period, I was leaving biology class and heading to algebra when I saw a large cluster of students gathered around a list that had been posted near the principal's office. Curious, I edged into the commotion. When I was close enough, I noticed the list was titled "Honor Roll" and ranked the top one hundred students in each grade. I wasn't aware that I would be ranked against the other students. I knew that there was an honor roll but not that there would actually be an ordered list of the top numerical grade point averages listed such that everyone could see it as they passed in front of the principal's office. As I glanced at the list, I noticed that in the freshman class listing, Lourdes Leal, a very intelligent Cuban-American girl, ranked first. Then as I looked down the list, I noticed that my name was in the third position, tied for second with a close friend, Yazid Ebeid. I knew that I had done well but was speechless that I had done that well. The other students in the top twenty were my classmates in the college prep courses. These were very talented kids, and I could not quite believe that I had surpassed so many. I was strangely moved at this affirmation of my work. However, I was not deceived into thinking that this made me superior to anyone else. I was honest with myself. I knew in my heart that many of these students were more talented than I was, but I was also convinced that no other student worked as hard as I did.

Just as I was starting to do really well in school, our lives suddenly came to a standstill on a cold day, December 5, 1982. My parents received a phone call telling them that Grandmother Alicia had died. My father's mother had been sick for months from heart failure brought on by her diabetes. In the last weeks, there were calls every few days from Aunt Gilma in Colombia telling us how much pain my grandmother was in and how much discomfort she was feeling. "You must come back," she told my father. "Mother is very sick, and she keeps losing weight. She doesn't have long to live. You should be at her bedside. She has not seen you in so many years, and this may be the last opportunity." My father felt very guilty and said to my mother, "I need to go back." Then he would talk on the phone with Grandmother Alicia and she would leave no doubt about what he must do. "You stay put in the United States," she insisted. "Make sure you don't come back. Think about your family. I'll be fine. My son, I beg you that you stay. I know that in spirit you will always be with me, even when I die. You must promise me that you will stay there."

My father knew he would risk everything if he returned—his family's wellbeing, his children's education, his job. The problem of undocumented immigrants was front-page news, and the United States government was clamping down. If he flew back, he might find it impossible to return unless he smuggled himself across the Mexican border by foot or in the trunk of a car—both were dangerous options given what he heard about the treacherous crossing from Mexico. The journey could be very expensive and possibly fatal. Although he was in great pain and anguish, he decided not to visit his ailing mother. Grandmother Alicia would have been very sad if she saw him return to Colombia just to see her die.

Then the phone call came that he had been dreading. We were sitting in the living room and we heard my father on the phone with Gilma and we knew from his face that Grandmother Alicia was gone. My father was so overcome that he gave the phone to my mother while he wrestled with the news, tears gathering in his eyes. "I have to go back now, for the funeral," he said, his voice very solemn. He sat on the sofa, crying, my mother trying to console him. My brother and I remained standing in a corner, quietly watching my parents and feeling pained that my father could not be with his mother when she passed on. We felt that we had abandoned my grandmother in her last few days.

A dark cloud seemed to descend on our small apartment. However, we were confident that my father knew that he could not go back. He soon rose to his feet and lit a candle next to a faded photograph of his mother. Over the next nine days, he went to church every day to say his novenas, lighting candles at another photograph of her that was adorned with flowers and a cross. It was the only way he could mark his mother's death. In an ironic twist of fates, that same night my parents had been called to come to Memorial High for their first parent-teacher conference that year. Somehow, my father was able to calm down and muster the courage to attend parents' night at the high school.

My father appeared like a beaten man. Despite all his successes so far, now he could not return to Colombia to see his mother one last time. Fortunately, the deep sadness and anguish was slightly diminished by his discussion with my teachers. On this sad night, my parents received uplifting evaluations from my teachers. One evaluation in particular was from an important role model for me. This was my biology teacher, Mr. Kirchmer. He was a young and energetic man who first introduced me to the beauty of living organisms in an elegant and colorful way. He spoke to my parents through a Spanish interpreter. Fortunately, the evaluations were all excellent.

With great excitement, Mr. Kirchmer said, "I wish my own son was as good as Harold." At some point, he even tried speaking some Spanish, telling my parents, "Hijo excelente."

My mother tried to restrain herself, to maintain her dignity and poise, but I could see tears begin to run down her face. She rose and gave Mr. Kirchmer a warm hug. All the sacrifices they had made, the years separated from their sons, the long days in the factories, the stern lectures every time we strayed into mischief, the sacrifice they made to abstain from visiting family when Grandmother Alicia was dying, were paying off. Their son was thriving in this new world. For my father, how painful for him it must have been that his mother could not be with him to share in his pride.

Nevertheless, my father took comfort in knowing that I was responding to his pleas that I work hard. When he returned from the conference, he knelt by his bed and thanked the Lord. He also thanked Grandmother Alicia for her sacrifice and compassionate understanding. He made copies of my report card, with the glowing teacher comments, and taped it to the inside of his locker at work. He was proud of my work and would often call over his colleagues and show them. Eventually, the door of his locker was filled with report cards, newspaper clippings, and other mementoes of my accomplishments.

"There are only two options: Make progress or make excuses."

—Inky Johnson

15.
Getting Started

"Create a spark of energy. Start with a simple task but do it really well."
—Harold Fernandez

When I heard the shrieking sound of the alarm clock, I pulled the warm blanket down from over my head, turned around in my bed, and reached over with my right hand to turn it off. I did not want the noise to wake up Byron or the rest of my family. After rubbing my eyes for a couple of seconds, I was able to look at the bright screen and I realized that it was 4:30 a.m. I sprung out of bed onto the cold floor of my room and rushed over to my closet. I quickly put on a pair of sweatpants and my heavy winter jacket, and then I put the bag that was hanging on the inside of the closet door on my shoulder and across my chest. As silently as I could, I tippy-toed across the kitchen floor and exited my apartment through the front door and came down one set of stairs to the lobby. Once I was outside my building, I started jogging to the apartment building on 57th Street and Boulevard East. It was a cold winter morning, and it had snowed the day before so there was still some snow on the street. But nothing was going to keep me from doing my job as a newspaper delivery boy for the *Hudson Dispatch* in Hudson County. I had decided to be the best newspaper boy in America.

I am not sure at what point or how exactly I decided to embark on this project. At some point early in my high school years, at the lowest point of my existence in America as an undocumented immigrant, I decided that it was a good idea for me to do a simple task. Something that I could do well. "What can I do, Lord?" I kept asking during my conversations with God. "What can I do to make things better?" I had seen Mama humiliated, and I had seen the working conditions for Papa. Now it was my turn to make something positive happen in my life. I thought that I could earn some spending money and that I could perhaps also help my parents. I decided to get a job delivering the newspaper. This would not take too much time out of my life, and I could do it early in the morning before school started so that it did not interfere with my classes or other activities. The biggest hurdle was to convince Papa to let me do it.

I approached him one night when he appeared to be in a good mood. It was after work, and he was busy watching the Yankees on television. They were winning, so he appeared content. I came into the living room and said, "Hey, Papa, can I ask you for a favor?" "Yes, my son, how can I help?" he responded. I said, "Papa, I've been thinking that it will greatly help me out if I could get a job delivering the newspaper." As Papa was about to answer, I said, "Look, Papa, I've been thinking that this will be good. I can make some money, and I promise you that my grades in school will improve." My father said, "You know, Harold, most kids that start to work never finish school, and I feel that school should be your number one priority." I responded, "Yes, Papa, yes, and I agree with you. But please, Papa, I promise that my grades will be better. If they are not, I will quit my job right away."

Papa noticed that I was in fact very serious about this, and he did not want to get in the way. Also, he had noticed that I had started to do better already in school. My grades were improving slowly, I was no longer getting in fights, I was no longer missing school, and I was spending my free time at home studying. He did not want to disappoint me. "Fine, Harold, let me speak with your mother, and I'll see what she says." But I had already discussed it with Mama. I had already convinced her that this was a good idea.

So the next day, Papa called me over and said, "Yes, Harold, we will allow you to get that job with two conditions: one, that you do not drop out of school, and two, that this doesn't affect your grades." With excitement, I said, "Thank you, Papa, thank you. I promise that my grades in school will be better. I promise, Papa. If not, I will quit."

So a few weeks later I started doing a paper route for our local paper, the Hudson Dispatch. I quickly developed a routine that did not interfere with my other activities. I would wake up at 4:30 in the morning, run from my house to the apartment complex on 57th and Boulevard East, pick up my bundle of papers there, and load them into my bag that I wore on the side hanging from my shoulder. I would take the elevator to the 26th floor and, looking at my list, drop off the paper at the door of each apartment. After delivering on all the twenty-six floors, I would then load the rest of the papers and move on to a couple of other smaller buildings, and then move to 59th street between Park Avenue and Broadway and deliver to the standalone houses. This would take me about fifty minutes to an hour.

On Thursday afternoons, I would go around collecting the money from my customers. My first time, I knocked on the door of the second-story house on Broadway. My brother Byron had accompanied me. He had decided to come with me, very excited to see his older brother in action doing a job in America. After a few seconds, my customer in the apartment said, "Who is it?" I was surprised, and I was not prepared with an answer. I looked at Byron as if looking for help, and then I turned and said, "This is your boy paper." It sounded awkward, so I turned again to Byron and noticed that he was laughing. I realized that I had made a grave error and repeated, "Sorry, your paper boy, your new paper boy." The lady opened the door and with a smile said, "So, you are the new paper boy?" I replied, "Yes, yes." She then reached for an envelope that she had within reach and handed it to me and said, "Thank you for the paper, and good luck with your route." I replied, "Thank you."

As we exited the house, Byron let out a bigger laugh, making fun of my accent and the way that I had mishandled my English. The fact was that although we were feeling more comfortable speaking the language, we still made many mistakes, and this made us very shy and self-conscious speaking to others in public. We walked out and opened the envelope to reveal the money for the paper and a one-dollar tip. I thought this was so great. If everyone gave us a tip, we could make a good amount of money each week.

After a few weeks, I realized that I enjoyed doing my paper route each day. I was able to exercise each day, start my day working, and then go home to take a shower and be ready for school. At some point, I also made a commitment that I was going to do this job so well that I would be the best newspaper boy in America. I would say to myself, "No one will be better than me in the United States." So I decided never to miss a day delivering the paper, even if it was snowing, or raining, or even if I was sick. No way, no how. That paper was always going to be there at the door of my customer in good condition. I also decided to ask my customers if they preferred to have the paper outside the door or if they wanted me to slip it underneath the door so they wouldn't have to open the door in the morning. I made a note of this on my list, but eventually I memorized it. Later, I started to be more interactive with my customers, friendly with a smile, and asked them about their neighbors to see if they wanted to get the paper as well. After about a year, I was able to increase my paper route from about ninety papers to 130 papers.

Then one day I got the biggest surprise of my life in America. My manager called me and informed me that I had been selected as the newspaper carrier of the month. I was ecstatic, especially when he said, "Make sure that you look at Saturday's paper because there will be an article about you." Sure enough, on Saturday as I kneeled down to pick up the bundle of papers, I opened one and saw the article there with my picture. The title was, "Harold Fernández, Newspaper Carrier of the Month." After I completed my route that day, I woke up my parents to show them the article. My parents were so happy. My papa cut out the article and placed it in his locker at work, and my mother put it in her purse and would show it to everyone, even people that she barely knew on Bergenline Avenue, saying, "Look, look, my son, my son!" That night, before going to bed, I felt an incredible amount of joy that I was doing something positive for me and for my humble parents. I couldn't get off my mind the image of the smile on Mama's face each time she showed that newspaper article to others. Slowly, I decided that I was going to use the same energy, enthusiasm, and passion for all my other activities. I started to see that with small changes in my life, big things could happen.

Another benefit of getting up so early and doing my paper route was that I had time to reflect and think about things in my life. As I walked, for example, I enjoyed reviewing some of my school lessons in my mind. I would review aloud formulas for my geometry class or algebra. But the best part was daydreaming. My mind would drift into thinking of one day being able to help my parents, or even maybe becoming a respected doctor. That simple paper route also provided the spark for another great activity in my early years in America.

On another cold winter morning, as I kneeled down to pick up the bundle of newspapers, my attention was captivated by a front-page photograph of students posing with medals around their necks and celebrating their scientific accomplishments at the annual science fair sponsored by the Stevens Institute of Technology. The small print under the picture listed the names of the students and referenced the page in the paper where one could find the article. With a rush of excitement, I ripped one of the papers out of the bundle and flipped to that page. I was filled with a spark of energy, fascination, and envy at the accomplishments of these kids. "Wow," I kept saying to myself. Little did I know that this rush of excitement that I felt would be a catalyst for my own personal journey into the art of investigation and scientific discovery. On this ordinary morning, as I delivered the papers, after briefly reading the article about the students in the science fair, I daydreamed about developing a project of my own. I was a stubborn kid. Whenever I had an idea, I had to make it happen. I stopped and read the article again. I was mesmerized that students my own age could do such sophisticated work. I sat down on the bundle of papers and started thinking about what I could possibly do. I started asking myself how I could do something like that so that I could be in the paper instead of delivering the paper.

The article said, "Stevens Institute in Hoboken, one of the top engineering schools in the Northeast, holds this contest each year to encourage high school students to pursue their interests in technological research and engineering." I was in the early months of my second year of high school, and right there and then I decided that I needed to do a project like the students in the photograph had done. I wasn't very inventive and didn't have anyone that I could come to for advice on planning this kind of research. My parents would not be of much practical help, since neither spoke English or had a scientific background. I could have asked for the help of one of my science teachers, all of whom were excellent, but as a relative newcomer to American society, I still didn't feel comfortable sharing my thoughts with them.

I only needed to find a project. For the next few months this became my foremost concern. I would repeatedly tell myself, "I need to do something!"

This is what I was thinking one December night in 1982 while I was walking down Bergenline Avenue, which was packed with crowds doing their holiday shopping. As I walked, shivering from the cold with my hands in my coat pockets, I briefly glanced at a window with computers. I had never had a computer. I had never seen or used a computer before, but I had seen all the commercials about using computers for playing video games. As I stood at the glass window, staring at these computers, I overheard a couple discussing the virtues of a Commodore computer on display. With great excitement, the wife explained to the husband how useful this machine could be for their kids' schoolwork. I don't know if the husband was really listening, but I was. She then proceeded to explain how their kids could even use this computer for school assignments and projects. When I heard the word "projects," I was in a daze. I instantly made the connection to my desire to enter a science fair competition. I thought that maybe, just maybe, I could use a computer, too, and I began to play with the thought that I could use a computer to develop a project for the Stevens Institute contest.

I rushed home thinking about computers. But I really did not know what they did or how they worked. I didn't even know how expensive they were. I wondered in my head if my parents could even afford to buy one.

The next time I passed the store, I gathered the courage to come inside and ask for information. The store clerk explained that the most popular computers were the Texas Instruments TI-94/A, the Commodore 64, and the IBM. He also explained that although all of them could be used to play games, they could also be used for schoolwork and for developing projects. Computers, I learned, were expensive. As I left the store, I realized my parents would be skeptical of spending so much on something that might be used for games that would distract me from my studies. Therefore, I had to come up with a plan.

I first mentioned the idea to Mama. I knew that she would be more receptive. I explained to her that I could use this computer for school. I also told her that I would save all my earnings from the paper route to help with the expense. My mother could sense the excitement that I had. She said yes immediately. "Of course, my son, let me talk it over with your father, and we will come up with the money." Upon hearing that I could use this for my education, my father also said yes, they would help me. My parents said that they would provide half the money for the least expensive of the three, the TI-94/A. I had saved enough from my earnings on the newspaper route to provide the remainder.

I got the TI-94/A computer on Christmas Eve of 1982, and it was love at first sight. By Colombian tradition, we celebrate on Christmas Eve, usually with Colombian food, dancing, and celebrating into the next morning. At midnight, we pause to open up the gifts by the Christmas tree. I couldn't wait to get my hands on the computer. As Mama distributed the gifts, she handed this one to me and said, "Enjoy it, my son. You deserve this and more." I took the box into my room with Byron and we ripped off the paper. I slid the computer out of the box and set it up on top of the television set in my room. The computer came with a detailed instruction manual and a book on BASIC computer language so that I could, if I read it meticulously, learn how to write programs. That first night, as everyone was partying and celebrating into the late morning—and as Byron was playing with other toys—I started teaching myself how to work this computer. For the next several weeks, I became addicted to these books, memorizing every detail and teaching myself computer language. I was mesmerized by the idea that one could talk to these machines and instruct them to do tasks. I started writing simple programs, and within a few weeks progressed to more complex ones. To the frustration of Byron, I rarely used the computer for playing games. I had a project to develop. Even to this day, he playfully reminds me that I stole part of his childhood. The next step, of course, was to actually design and develop an idea. As I taught myself the language of computers, my mind was also consumed with trying to figure out a project. Each morning when I opened my eyes, and each night when I went to bed, I would be preoccupied thinking of what project I could possibly do for the science fair.

"The most important investment you can make is in yourself."

—Warren Buffet

16.
A Small Step

"You can make anything happen if you concentrate on small steps and you tackle one obstacle at a time."
—Harold Fernandez

One ordinary morning, as I was sitting quietly on my chair, trying to copy the notes that my general chemistry teacher was writing on the blackboard, I suddenly had an idea for my science fair project. Mr. Thomas Simione had been a teacher of general chemistry at Memorial for many years, and I could sense that he had lost some of his understanding of the material. He was a good teacher, but over the years he had lost some interest. He could copy the lesson from his well-kept notes onto the chalkboard, but he could not explain it to the students. One lesson that sparked my interest was his explanation of the "electron cloud." He would get up in front of the board, pick an element from the periodic table, and copy from his notes the electronic configuration of the electrons on the board. However, he could not explain it to us in a way that we could actually understand. As I looked at the board, I got the idea that this would be my project. I said to myself, "I will teach myself everything there is to know about the electron cloud, and I will write a program that teaches other students how to do it in a simple way."

Each element has a specific number of electrons surrounding the nucleus, and theories by Niels Bohr and Max Planck use mathematical formulas to pinpoint the configuration of the electrons—the precise positions and pattern of the electrons that orbit the central nucleus. I wrote a program to teach students how to make calculations to figure out the electronic configuration for themselves. The title of my project was *Application of Computers to Chemistry*, and it had two other sections that also aimed to illustrate how a computer could be used to get across concepts in chemistry. There was a complex graphics program that simulated an experiment showing how the organic compound chloral hydrate is produced. There was also a tool that was designed to teach students how to calculate nuclear binding energy of several atoms by using the concept of mass defect and Einstein's equation of $E=mc^2$.

It took me several months of intensive labor to write this program. Because I didn't have any formal training in computers, I am sure that some of the algorithms I used were not optimal. Nevertheless, I finished the entire project on my own. I didn't ask anyone for help or advice. One hundred percent of the work was derived from my ideas and my own labor. Although it was not perfect, I was very proud of the final result. I entered my project in the Stevens Institute Science Fair for 1984, my junior year. After preliminary rounds that took a few weeks, I received a letter telling me that my project had been selected as a finalist and would be displayed to the judges. I was ecstatic.

On the day of the final competition, I had the opportunity to see the other projects and meet the other competitors. There were ten finalists, mostly students from Indian and Chinese immigrant homes. I could not help noticing that I was the only Hispanic student. I also could not help noticing that parents accompanied each student, with many of the fathers in jackets and ties and the mothers in elegant dresses. My parents were not able to make it to the contest. They needed to work. Their factories didn't even allow them any sick days. My parents did not have any legal documents to be here in America. They realized that they could be fired from their jobs even if they missed one day of work. Yet my parents' faces glowed with pride at what I was doing.

"Oh, my son, we are so proud of you, of all this wonderful work that you are doing because you work so hard," my mother told me. My father, in particular, knew that I was doing something special because it was related to Albert Einstein. My father esteemed that name, even if he had no understanding of relativity or quantum physics.

So on the day of the competition, I was alone with my TI-94/A computer. Most of the other finalists were dressed in suits and ties. I was more casually dressed in jeans and a neat and comfortable shirt. The other students used more advanced and expensive computers, IBM or Commodore-64 models, that allowed storage on floppy disks. My project was saved on an ordinary cassette tape, and to play it I had to attach a tape recorder to my computer. I imagined the other students and their parents thinking, "How can this kid possibly be competing with his toy computer?" Each time that I loaded my program, it would take ten to fifteen minutes to start. A judge would come by and ask to see my project, and I would have to ask him or her to look at another project first and return in ten minutes. At other times, I would try to distract the judge with an expanded verbal explanation of my project to allow time for the program to boot. Still, by the afternoon, I felt that the judges understood that my project was an original idea and, just as important, that I had done the work on my own, without any assistance from teachers or parents. At the end of the day, the judges met and announced the top three finishers in each category. I finished in third place in my category.

A few weeks later, I received a letter from Rensselaer Polytechnic Institute (RPI) that invited me to apply to their annual summer program for high school students in math and science. The school had been told that I had participated in the Stevens Science Fair and placed well. RPI, in Troy, in upstate New York, is one of the country's top engineering schools. The eight-week summer program offered two college-level courses in computer science: Introduction to Minicomputers and Computer Fundamentals 101. Each course covered an entire semester's work in a four-week period.

After reading the course description, I was fascinated at the thought of attending this summer program. But there was one major problem: it was very expensive. The cost of the program was about one third of what my parents made in one year. There was no way that they could afford this expense. I did what I knew how to do. I sent RPI many letters explaining my situation and my desire to attend the program. As best as I could, I put my heart into these letters, and I begged for the opportunity to attend. Someone at the other end was paying attention; a few weeks later, I was surprised to receive a letter admitting me and granting me a full financial aid package. I showed the letter to my parents, and they were astonished. My father could not believe that this was possible. He thought that I was not reading the letter correctly. I, too, had doubts that this could be true and wondered if someone had made an error. However, I soon understood that I was the beneficiary of American generosity at its best. I had received the trust of the admissions committee. Now I would need to show the school that I deserved the opportunity.

That summer of 1984, after my junior year of high school, would be the first time that I would leave my home for anything longer than a weekend Scout outing. We planned the trip to RPI carefully. In total, about ten people accompanied me to Troy. After all, my spending a summer at RPI was a monumental event for my wider family, and everyone wanted to witness it. None of them had ever spent any time on a college campus, but they understood that a university was a place of distinction. The idea that a young member of our humble family had been given the opportunity to travel and study at a university was a change in their conception of themselves.

For weeks before we left, my RPI summer became the talk of the town within my parents' circle of friends. The idea that now I was going to spend an entire summer at a university outside of West New York gave all of us hope that things could be better. Someone just like them was going to study with some of the country's best students. They all wanted to be part of the journey; they didn't want to be left out.

We made it to the campus without any breakdowns. That day at the dorm, there was a luncheon for the program's students and their families. Most students had come with their parents. I had come with my entire family: parents, brothers, uncle, cousins, and dog. It was obvious at the gathering which one was the immigrant Hispanic family. My brothers were running around, yammering in Spanish, and my mother was silently sobbing because I would be away from home for a whole summer. Being more practical, my father was preoccupied with making sure that we had not misunderstood the financial aid letter and that I would actually be able to afford to stay at the school. Otherwise, he might have to return to fetch me. He urged me to inquire about the letter at the registrar's office.

There was a line of students and their parents who, we could see, were signing forms and then going over to the cashier's desk and taking out checkbooks to pay the bill. My father, standing alongside me, was nervous because he didn't have a checkbook and had no idea how he was going to pay any fees that might be required. I registered and then moved to the cashier's desk, but instead of having to write a check, I was handed a check by the clerk, a stipend for books and supplies. My father was relieved, and we returned to the luncheon to enjoy a few moments together as a family before they would have to leave me on my own and drive back to West New York. My father was anxious about driving at night and so could only stay a couple of hours.

RPI was my first immersion in a solidly American environment. The program's forty students hailed from as far away as California, but there was only one other Hispanic, a student from a wealthy Puerto Rican family who had attended a private school in his homeland. Each of the courses was designed around a project using a different computer language—BASIC, FORTRAN, or PASCAL. The material was far more advanced than the programs I had used just a few months before at the science fair. We spent about six hours a day in the classroom, and each day we had programming assignments that were due the next day. The other students that summer also seemed much further along in their computer skills than me, but I also understood that I shared something very fundamental with all of them. All these students wanted to score well in the courses—you could see it in their eyes—and I, too, was there to do well. In fact, I probably wanted to do better than most of them because it was more important for me. Coming from a relatively unknown high school, a positive effort at RPI would improve my chances of getting noticed by a good college. Because I was far behind in computer skills, I had to work even harder and learn from my classmates.

The school made sure that we had access to several teaching assistants, and I was not embarrassed to show up at the cafeteria after dinner for daily tutoring sessions. I knew that at the end of the course, my transcript would only show my grade; it wouldn't have an asterisk indicating that I had obtained special tutoring. I was never ashamed to ask my roommate or other students for help. I was grateful that the students, even if they viewed me as a rival, were willing to explain difficult concepts.

I realized early on that I was different from the other students—

my accent, my culture, my interests, even my preferences in food made me stand out. The dorm cafeteria served American food: burgers, pizza, macaroni and cheese, and roast beef. After a few weeks, I longed for my mother's cooking—the rice, beans, *tostones, and arepas.* While Michael Jordan and the American basketball team's feats in the 1984 Summer Olympics captivated other students, I was perfecting my computer projects. I took only a few breaks, mostly to run a few miles each day or kick around a soccer ball to keep in shape for the fall season. Still, I found this taste of college and the freedom to be on my own liberating and exhilarating. I could study in a beautiful library on a table of my own with no salsa or merengue blasting from across the alley.

During this summer, I managed to really concentrate on my schoolwork. A few times during that summer, we went into town on weekends, mostly to a Friendly's restaurant. But my budget was very tight, and I couldn't afford even those meals. When my friends asked me to go, I would make up an excuse and say I had to study. Most days the real reason was I did not have the money. At times, I had a feeling that the other students considered me something of a loner. Undoubtedly, I felt that I did not quite belong in this program. I was an undocumented immigrant with a heavy accent and didn't even have enough money to join them at the local restaurants. I realized that I had many obstacles in front of me, and I decided that I would just concentrate on one of them, my schoolwork.

The hard work I put in was rewarded. I earned A's in both of my courses. When I returned home from Troy, I rode a bus into Grand Central Station in Manhattan. As I was sitting on this bus, I thought about the sequence of events that started with a simple idea as I picked up the bundle of newspapers to deliver. It was facilitated by the money that I earned with a humble job of delivering newspapers and by the generosity of an academic institution like RPI. "This is great, I love America," I whispered to myself. But even more important, this was further confirmation of how tiny steps can really change the direction of your life.

"Passion is a choice. You need to choose to be great. It is not a chance, it's a choice."

—Eliud Kipchoge

17.
Believing

"Don't be afraid to believe, it may change your life."
—Harold Fernandez

As a freshman, I had the fortune to fall in love, not with a girl, but with running. It all started on a cold, breezy November day, when we met for the first day of practice for the indoor track team. I had decided that I wanted to be a runner. I had just finished the fall season and done well on the soccer team, but I wanted to try another sport. We met at the high school gym and changed into running clothes. We started our practice by running two miles to the track field at the Hudson County Park. After we rested for a few minutes, our coach, Sal Vega, appeared with a group of six to seven of the elite runners on the team. They had just completed a three-mile run. These guys looked sharp. They were dressed in what appeared to me like professional running clothes and were sporting brand-new Adidas and Nike running shoes. This group of runners had just won the Hudson County Cross Country Championship. Coach Vega gave us a pep talk and then divided us into two groups: freshmen and the rest. He wanted to know what he was working with. We would have a practice mile race.

I was blown away by the speed of the race. The upperclassmen were coming in at around 4:40. I remember being nervous. I had not been running for several months, except for what I had done in soccer practice. I was already tired from the run to the park, I did not have running shoes, and several of the other runners had been part of the cross-country team during the summer and fall. My fear of coming in last was realized as I trailed the pack with a time of 5:30. As I approached the last turn of the race, I pushed as hard as I could, but it wasn't good enough. I was in last place. Not a great start, I thought. I was devastated. I was developing a competitive mind, and I was very upset at this result. My only consolation was that I had worked hard and managed to stay close to the pack. I was depressed at my performance and at the thought of having to run another two miles back to the high school.

After I had changed and was walking out of the locker room, disheartened and with my head down, I was called in to see Coach Vega. As I approached him, he said, "Harold, great job. I loved the way you hung in there." I could not believe what he had said. I thought, "Is he confusing me with someone else?" He was actually complimenting me on being last. In reality, he was complimenting me on having pushed myself and not given up. He saw that I was a fighter and that, with the right training, I could do well.

I was relieved that this important coach was taking the time to speak with me, a freshman who had just finished last in the tryout race. He must have seen something that I did not see, because he told me that he was very happy with my performance. In a very short period of time, I realized that Coach Vega was a special person. We had to call him by his first name, "Sal." He practiced with us every day. He took an interest in our families and in our performance in school. His team of runners was not just average—they were all superb competitors. The Memorial High School track and field team was one of the top programs in the state of New Jersey for many years. Our team was a family with a high amount of respect for our coach, a great person who led by example. I have always wondered how many kids in the barrios and ghettos of America would benefit from meeting a coach like this. His goal was to make me believe in myself through hard work and practice.

Every day that I went to train, I felt fortunate that I had met the right person to motivate me and inspire me as a runner. After four years of hard work, I had my best race in the outdoor season of my senior year. It was the half-mile race at the Hudson County championship, two laps around the track at a blazing pace. I felt ready. On the last lap, the bell rung. It was so loud. My body and legs felt heavy, almost as if I had bricks attached to my legs and arms. My breathing was heavy. I felt as if I had no control, and I wanted to stop. But deep within me, I could hear Coach Vega screaming, "You've got to stay close; you have to push your body." And so I did. I was exactly in the position that Coach Vega wanted. He did not want me to be in first place or in last place. He just wanted me to be close to the leader. It was a tight race with three much taller African American kids leading the pace. Next, I had to make a move, and I did. I pushed my body, brought in my elbows close to my sides, and lifted up my knees, keeping pace with the leaders. As the last hundred yards of the race approached, I gathered enough momentum to overtake the leaders all the way to the finish line, crossing in a time of just under two minutes. Not a meet record, or even a record at my school, but good enough to have won the gold medal. I felt ecstatic. I could see my coach a few feet away jumping up and down, celebrating as much as I was. I had finally listened to him. I had followed his instructions, and it was worth it. I had shown myself that with passion and hard work, anything is possible. I was definitely not the most talented runner, but on this day, I had the biggest heart.

As a child, I had never had an interest in running as a sport. My only interest had been soccer. I had lived my life playing soccer most of the day on the paved streets of Barrio Antioquia. I continued with this sport here in America, and then I discovered the joy and the thrill of competitive running. In fact, at Memorial, both soccer and running would become part of my life. In the fall, I played on the soccer team and ran cross country one year. In the winter, I ran for the indoor track team, and in the spring, I ran for the outdoor track team. There was probably not one day during my high school career that I was not either practicing soccer or running.

I learned many lessons from my time as a runner, including the importance of hard work, daily routines, passion, dedication, and the joy of winning, as well as how to learn and accept when you lose. As I runner, I also had the opportunity to fall in love with a dream and an idea of one day being a student at one of the top universities in the world. As a sophomore, I had qualified for the indoor state championships, which were always held in the majestic Jadwin Gym at Princeton University. Until then, I knew very little about this place, except that this was the university selected by Albert Einstein when he had escaped Nazi control.

The day of the meet was cold. We had just been through a huge snowstorm. The trip to Princeton from West New York took around three hours. We left early in the morning and arrived there at nine thirty. Upon exiting the bus, we were all captivated by the sight of this huge domed complex. The inside was even more impressive. It was clean, dry, spacious, and the track was beautifully maintained. This was in sharp contrast to our usual indoor track for the local county competition, which was held at the armory in Jersey City. It was much smaller, always humid, foggy, and had a wooden track floor. At times, it was so cloudy that you could not see the entire field from the stands. Sometimes you couldn't even see the runner in front of you. At the armory, we had to stay indoors the entire day because of concerns about the safety of some of the surrounding streets. But at Princeton's majestic campus we felt safe.

After the race, we exited for a short three-mile run on campus. This was the first time that I had seen such an astonishing place. I was overwhelmed by the stunning gothic structures, the appearance of the students walking across campus, and the well-maintained fields. The four of us who had participated in the two-mile relay race moved across the campus as a unit, making small talk, telling jokes, and admiring our surroundings. As I jogged around the campus and gazed at the dormitories, the libraries, and other academic buildings, I would dream about being a student there. My friends on the team who knew that I was a good student would shout, "Look, Harold, look! This can be your school." I would reply, "No way, guys, you all are crazy. This place is not for me."

But that is not what I was thinking in my mind and feeling in my heart. Although it first seemed such an impossible accomplishment, slowly I started to think, "Why not?" For the first time I started to tell myself, "I am not any different from the students here." I started to wonder, "Why can't I be a student at Princeton?" As I asked myself that question—"Why not?"—I sincerely started to believe that I could actually make it happen.

At the conclusion of the meet, we returned to our bus. It was already late into the night, and darkness had covered the surroundings. I climbed into the bus and found a seat near the back. I took out some of my clothes from inside my gym bag and made a small pillow in preparation for the three-hour ride back to West New York. The snowfall had been heavy, and I was sure that it was going to be a slow ride home. As the bus exited the parking lot, I could once again see the imposing dome-like shape of Jadwin Gym from the side, the beautiful historic Palmer Stadium, and then some of the other athletic fields in the background. I looked back as we drove away, repeating in my head, "Why not?"

During my ride back, I reflected on my life in America. My situation had changed so drastically in just a few years. I went from been a troubled teenager drinking alcohol to a young man dreaming of a better future at the top university in America. I had worked very hard and made many advances in my life. For better or for worse, I was starting to gain confidence about my academic abilities. When we reached the school that night, I had convinced myself that I needed to speak with my guidance counselor because I wanted to make plans to attend college. Slowly, I was becoming confident in my abilities and starting to believe in myself.

"The mind is everything. What you think, you become."
—Buddha

***"You don't become what you want,
you become what you believe."***
—Oprah Winfrey

18.
Daring to Dream

"Don't be afraid to dream big, despite what others might say or obstacles in front of you."
—Harold Fernandez

I didn't waste any time. I was feeling confident after having attended the track meet at Princeton. I wanted to talk to my guidance counselor about my desire to attend a university. The next morning, before classes, I walked over to her office and set up an appointment. I wanted to make sure that I was doing everything possible to get into my dream school. The day of the appointment I was so nervous, but I was ready to tell her about everything that I had done, and also that I was interested in Princeton University. With my palms sweaty and my legs trembling, I walked in and sat outside her office until I was called in to see her.

She called me in, and I sat next to her desk. She took out a folder and opened it. After a few minutes, she looked up at me and said that she was very happy with my record and that I shouldn't have any problems getting into school. We discussed the next steps. "Great, Harold, now you have to work hard and get ready for your SATs and then begin to apply to many special places." She then made a list of colleges that would be a good fit for me and explained why they would be a good fit. In the list, she included some of the local community colleges in Northern New Jersey, St. Peters College, Jersey City State College, and others. And then she said, "But I am confident that if you continue to do well, you will also get into Rutgers University." She did not even mention Princeton. I was completely quiet. I knew that Rutgers was an excellent university, but it was not where I had my dreams set on. There was probably no mention of Princeton because no one in the history of my school had ever been accepted to Princeton.

We had discussed that I had an interest in entering the medical field, and she said, "You know, Harold, all these schools have very good science departments, and you can take the courses there for medical school." I nodded my head in agreement as she continued her advice. But inside I was distraught that she had not mentioned the school of my dreams. I did not want to bring it up because I was not ready to have her disagree with me and tell me that my chances were in fact very low to get in. As I exited, I turned to her and said, "Thank you, Mrs. Perez, I appreciate your time and your advice."

As I walked out of the office, I felt as if the weight of the world was falling on me. My head and shoulders were down, and with a heavy heart I managed to start a slow walk through the main corridor to my classroom. I had not even brought up my desire to apply to Princeton and other Ivy League schools. I was embarrassed. I thought that she would laugh at me. I was convinced that after she looked at my record, she would recommend that I apply to the top schools in the country. I was wrong. For some reason, she was not as impressed with my record as I was. I whispered to myself, "What can I do, Lord?"

The bell had just rung, and the other students were slowly filling the halls as they rushed to get to their lockers and then to their next class. I slowly made my way to my locker and picked up my book. I asked myself, "Why I am feeling like this? I should be happy. I am the number one student at this school, and I have done so many other things." As the minutes passed, I actually became more energized and determined that this conversation with my guidance counselor was not going to discourage me from following my dreams. I decided that I was going to go ahead with my plans to apply to Princeton and some of the other top schools in the country. The words of others were not going to hold me back.

But there was a bigger problem that might, and I did not have any control over it. As much as I tried not thinking about it, I was alarmed that my status in America as an undocumented immigrant might be an insurmountable hurdle. Over the next few months, I started making a detailed plan about how I was going to apply to college. I realized that Mama and Papa, or anyone else in my family, were not going to be of much help as no one in my family had ever applied to or attended a university. Papa had dropped out of school in first grade, and Mama had barely made it through third grade. I knew that I was going to be filling out many forms and letters on my own. For convenience, I even learned how to copy my parents' signatures so that I didn't bother them each time I had to fill out a form.

When I had free time, I would often run over to the WNY public library on 60th Street. I spent many hours there reading books. I liked this library because unlike at home, this place was very quiet, and you could always find a little corner or space and read books in peace. But now as I was starting to plan for a college education, I spent many hours reading books about different schools and the process of applying to college. But my interest and fascination always came to Princeton. I fell in love with their school handbook. I would look at the pictures of the campus with its beautiful magical gothic buildings, the history of Albert Einstein, the many Nobel Prize winners, and their many athletic teams. I also read other books that described stories of Albert Einstein walking around campus and explaining lessons to students. I was fascinated by the magic and the history of this place. The pictures in the handbook made it look like an enchanted castle teeming with school spirit, magical adventures, and the best possible education.

Nonetheless, I made a list of several schools, including Brown, RPI, Yale, Rutgers, Caltech, and Princeton. In a separate small notebook that I titled "My College Dream," I made elaborate notes about each school. My notes included specific details about their faculty, student life, academics, and soccer programs, and also the addresses of the admissions office. I then sent letters to each school requesting an application. As the applications started to come in, I realized that I was going to have a problem. In each application, there was a space for a social security number, and there was always a question about citizenship or permanent residency. Some of the schools also wanted a photocopy of my green card. For several days and weeks, I wrestled with this problem. I didn't have any of these documents. I needed to find a solution, otherwise I would not be going to college. For many nights I couldn't fall asleep worrying and agonizing about what to do. I decided to discuss it with my parents.

The next time we gathered at our kitchen table to have dinner, I said, "Papa, I have been reading about colleges and getting their applications because I really want to go to college, but there is a problem because I don't have a green card or social security card." My papa and mama were taken aback, and they seemed very distraught and sad. "Yes, my son," said Papa, "we have been talking about this for a while, me and your mother, and we have been asking around to find a solution." I was relieved that I was not alone and happy that my parents had been thinking about this as well and trying to find a solution.

The real problem was that there was not much that they could do. They had been trying for years to legalize their status here without any success. Many visits to immigration lawyers had not been helpful. In one instance, a lawyer that my parents saw in Union City told Mama, "Lady, you are lucky that you are still here, and please go and hide." He was basically saying that there was no way for my family to become legal in America, and therefore there was no easy way for me to get the necessary documents.

But there was another way. My parents had received information from friends of people who could manufacture a counterfeit green card for a fee. Through a series of contacts, we found a person who sold them for $250. The document, my parents were told, would be an exact replica of a real one and it would have my picture on it. The only way to know that it wasn't real was to check the number against the central INS database—but who would go through that trouble? Although we all struggled with the decision to do this, we realized that this was the only way for me to be able to even apply to college. We also decided that we would only use this document for getting my social security card and for my applications. We would not use it for any other public or private matters.

When the green card was delivered two weeks later, I examined it carefully. Although I had never seen a real one before, I sensed that this card appeared phony. Nonetheless, I didn't have much of a choice. I would need to use it for college applications and also to obtain a genuine social security number at a social security office. We were advised not to visit the local office in West New York. With so many immigrants in town, the clerks there were quite familiar with forged green cards.

Instead, we were urged to visit an office in a smaller New Jersey town without a large immigrant population.

One of the places recommended was the town of Long Branch on the central New Jersey coast. So I decided to make my way to that town. I didn't have anyone who could drive me there, and therefore I decided to use New Jersey Transit. On a boiling, humid August day in 1983, between my junior and senior years of high school, I took a bus from West New York to the bus terminal in Manhattan, and then another bus to Long Branch. The bus station in Long Branch was two miles from the local social security office, and I had to walk the entire way.

When I reached the office, I was sweating profusely. It was not just from the heat, but also from anxiety and desperation about what I was about to do. I was now in an office of the United States government and about to present the officials there with a forged document. When the lady at the desk saw that I was drenched, she offered me a glass of water. I gladly took it and informed her that I was there to apply for a social security card. I told her that I lived in West New York, but that I had a summer job in the Long Branch area. She took some of my information and then asked me to come inside where a second clerk would finish processing the application. She then asked me for my green card. Trembling, I reached into my wallet and put the card on her desk. She glanced at it briefly, put it back on the desk, and then left for an office nearby.

From where I was sitting, I could see that she was making telephone calls. I was too far away to figure out the nature of her calls, but after a few minutes of waiting, I became convinced that she was calling the Immigration and Naturalization Service to check on the green card's authenticity. I was growing more anxious by the second. I could no longer tolerate the tension and decided that I would make an escape. When it appeared that she was not looking in my direction, I picked up my green card and all the other documents that I had filled out, and I walked out of the office. No one saw me, and I made an uneventful exit. Once outside, I didn't run, but I strode as fast as I could to the bus station and returned home two hours later.

I was disheartened that I still didn't have a social security card, but happy that I had been able to escape without any major problems. I realized then that I did not have the strength to present this forged document to anyone in person.

Over the next few weeks, the deadlines for submitting college applications approached. We asked friends for other means of getting a social security number and learned of a worker at one of the federal offices who, for a small fee, would process an application for a valid number. I would be getting a card actually printed by the Social Security Administration, and the worker would not ask to see a residency card. This worker let me obtain a social security card with an apparently legitimate number. I was ecstatic. This was the last hurdle that had prevented me from filling out my applications. I was now free to apply to the university of my dreams. I could now dare to dream, and I now had the confidence to dream big.

"If you can dream it, you can do it."
—Walt Disney

19. A Miracle

"I hope that each student graduating here tonight never gives up, for failure only exists in the mind."
—Harold Fernandez

On a warm spring day in early March of 1984, I rushed home after my track and field practice. I was exhausted as I reached home. For the last few days, there was only one thing on my mind. Every night, I asked God for a miracle, "Oh, Lord, please give me the opportunity to attend this beautiful university." I was completely preoccupied with whether or not I would get an admission letter from Princeton University. As I entered the lobby of our apartment building, I climbed the stairs up to the second floor to apartment 3B. Without knocking, I opened the front door to the pleasant aroma of Mama's freshly cooked rice and beans. Thrilled to see me, she said, "Hi, my son, how was your day?" I replied, "Mama, have you picked up the mail yet?" She answered, "No, my son, I have not." Mama realized that I was very stressed out and worried because I had been waiting to receive my letter from Princeton. Every day I came home from school, picked up the keys to our mailbox, and sprinted down the stairs to see if the letter had arrived. That was exactly what I did now. But for some reason, I had a feeling that the letter would arrive today. All day in school, I had been imagining and thinking about opening this letter. I had already received letters of acceptance to Yale, Brown, Cornell, University of Pennsylvania, RPI, and Rutgers, and I was turned down by the California Institute of Technology. I should have been very happy, but in my heart, my dream was to be accepted to Princeton. From my acceptance letters and also from hearsay, I had learned that rejection letters came in small envelopes. Acceptance letters, on the other hand, come in large envelopes because they were accompanied with other documents, such as financial aid forms or orientation documents. I was certainly hoping to see a large envelope.

As I put in the key to open the mailbox, I glanced through the small slits of the door and I could just make out the black and orange colors of the Princeton logo on a small envelope. This was confirmed when I finally opened it and took out all the mail. I felt the wind knocked out of me as if someone had just hit me in my stomach. With a sense of desolation, I whispered to my soul, "Oh, Lord, it's a small envelope. I've been denied." I did not have the courage to open the envelope. Somehow, although I really had no energy, I managed to slowly walk upstairs, a beaten man, and rushed through the kitchen. I wanted to be invisible and not to be seen by anyone, even my mama. I handed the rest of the mail to her and kept the Princeton letter with me. My mama said, "My son, are you okay?" I replied as I closed the door to my room, "Yes, Mama, I am fine, I just have a lot of work to do." My mama realized that I was not fine. She knew exactly what I had been waiting for, and how much this meant to me. She wanted to sit me down and show me love and tell me that everything was going to be fine, but she was afraid and wanted to let me be on my own.

Inside my bedroom, I sat down on the edge of the bed, just looking at this envelope. For several minutes I thought about all the things that I had accomplished in my short stay in America. I told myself that just a few years earlier, I did not even speak a word of English, and I was getting into daily fights in school, smoking cigarettes with my friends, and drinking hard liquor on warm summer days. I recalled that visit with Mama to the vice-principal's office when she was warned that I might be suspended from school, and also recalled how this moment had changed my attitude and my determination to change my life. In my head I recalled all the things that I had done so far in America, including my triumph in the track stadiums, the soccer fields, the Boy Scouts, my A-grades during my two college-level courses at RPI, and, of course, my rank as the number one student in my high school. I slowly realized that I had nothing to be ashamed about and nothing to fear. Nonetheless, there was a part of me that searched for perhaps something that I could have done differently, or better. But the more I thought, the more I realized that I had done everything possible and that I should celebrate everything that I had accomplished so far in my short stay here in America.

I finally mustered the courage to open the envelope and read the letter. The letter started with the sentence, "The admissions committee is pleased to inform you that you have been accepted to the graduating class of 1989 at Princeton University…" After reading this, I was in a state of unparalleled joy. I yelled loud enough for the entire building to hear me. "Mama, Mama, I've been accepted to Princeton. I cannot believe this, Mama." My mother stopped everything she was doing to stop me, look me in the eyes, and say, "Wow, my son, this is great news. You should be very proud. This is a great accomplishment. I will call your papa right away."

As Mama moved over to make the phone call, I slipped around her and I sprinted out of the apartment. I was ecstatic, and I had so much energy that I needed to let it out. I went out for a three-mile jog to Hudson County Park. This was how I celebrated my admission to the university of my dreams. During my jog, I recalled that cold winter night in 1982 at the indoor state championships at Princeton when I went for a warm-down jog with my teammates around the campus and had a vision of becoming a student here, and how this vision led to a strong belief in my heart that I could make this happen.

My father was perhaps even more enthusiastic than I was when he received the call from Mama. He could not believe it. Although he was not an expert on college admissions, he knew that this was a gigantic accomplishment. He had often heard of Princeton in the news as the university where the great genius Albert Einstein had been a professor, and more recently he had heard that this was the school also chosen by the great child actress prodigy, Brooke Shields. My papa was very reserved, and he often kept things to himself, but this was something that he had to share with others. So after hanging up on the phone with Mama, he rushed over to tell his boss and his co-workers. I think that his boss may not have been as thrilled because he asked Papa, "Are you sure, Alberto? Are you sure that this is the university, or maybe it is a community college in Princeton?" My papa let it go. He clearly understood that this was a miracle and that others might not believe him. But the important part was that his son was happy.

Although I had been accepted to some of the best universities in the country, including Yale, Brown, and Cornell, the decision of where to enroll was easy. My mind was made up, and I decided to attend Princeton University. Every night I would fall asleep reading the school handbook and imagining myself as a student there walking along the narrow tree-lined paths that connect the ancient gothic buildings, including its main administration building, Nassau Hall, which at one point had been army barracks that housed George Washington and his soldiers.

The next step was to fill out the enrollment forms. Each time that I sat down at our small dinner table with my parents to fill out these forms, I was reminded of how vulnerable and delicate my status in America was. Many nights at this dinner table, with my parents next to me, we agonized about a few of the questions that asked for the social security card and for copies of my residency card. We had tried so hard to legalize our status in America and to obtain these documents, but we could not. As I flipped through the different forms, I would pause each time this information was required and look at Mama and Papa. Without words, and only as if moved by our necessity, I would then fill out the numbers that I had from the documents that we had purchased. Realizing how difficult this was, my papa would often say, "Try not to think about this, son. I know that this is hard, but this is the only way for you to be able to go to the university and follow your dreams of helping others."

As my papa was finishing his explanation, my mama would reach over and put her hand on my shoulder and nod her head as well in approval. After receiving their approval, I would then complete the forms, place them in the envelopes, and put them on a corner so that I could bring them to the mailbox the next day. Despite getting their approval, however, there were many nights that I went to bed fearing the worst. I would toss and turn in bed thinking, "What if someone finds out?" I would ask myself, "What would happen if they ask me to show them my green card?" Would I be able to do it? Or would I turn away like I had done a few months earlier at the social security office in Long Branch? Honestly, I did not know, but I did know that this was my only chance of getting an education, and I realized that I had to put my faith in God that it would all work out fine.

Finally, on a hot summer day in June of 1985, I heard my name being called to receive my high school diploma. I carefully made my way around the chairs on the stage and walked over to meet Mr. Vanzanten, the new principal. He extended his hand and gave me the diploma. I told him thanks, and then I raised my hand in the direction of where my parents were sitting. This was such a special night for me. I was also receiving the award as the valedictorian of my high school, and then my name was called to give the valedictorian speech. It was such an incredible honor and privilege to address my classmates, parents, and friends, as well as the teachers and administrators. I had never spoken in front of so many people before. This was Miller Stadium, where the football team led by Principal Coviello played, and today it was packed to the rim with parents and friends. I almost felt as if I did not have control of my legs as I walked up to the podium. I had carefully written a speech that I felt could inspire the students to know that this was the start of our lives, that they could do better and also that they could "let free those cells in their hearts that hunger for justice." As I approached the podium, I thought of my grandmothers, and I gained strength and courage to deliver my words. I put the paper on the podium, and in a slow and firm voice speaking though the microphone with my heavy accent, I delivered the following speech:

Tomorrow we join humanity in its search for the ultimate truth—that which is the key to an ideal society where there is no evil and no fear of war. Let each graduate take a step toward the ultimate truth by developing his or her own character. Let free that part of our minds that hungers for knowledge and let free those cells in our heart that hunger for justice and love. Character is the soul of happiness, just as 'brevity is the soul of wit.' It is that unit that measures how close we are to real success. Tonight, we should also reflect on our performance at Memorial. Even though some of us have not worked to our potential, we still have an opportunity for a new beginning—a commencement. The mistakes we may have made in our last four years can be utilized to our advantage. Trying to reach the best of our abilities is all we can ask of ourselves, for human resources are endless and our best is always enough. I hope that each student graduating here tonight never gives up, for failure only exists in the mind. Thank you."

I received a tremendous applause from my classmates and from the crowd. As I ended my remarks, I paused for a second and then thought of my grandmothers again. I needed more courage to do the next step. I flipped over the page, and I started to deliver a few thoughts in my native language, Spanish. As I did, the entire stadium stood up and listened to all my words. Then at the conclusion, I received a standing ovation. Many parents were crying. I had connected with my people. I had connected with a huge community of immigrant parents and family members who clearly love America but also feel a deep and strong connection to their native land and to their language. But even more important, they felt a strong connection with our struggles and dreams here in America as immigrants, especially when I thanked "my Grandmother Alicia who is in Heaven." As immigrants, many of them, including my own father, had lost dear family members that they had not seen for many years. We connected because we had so much in common, and many parents were visibly moved.

We celebrated the night of my graduation with a mass at home. Mama had asked the local priest to come by to bless my graduation and also to bless my desire to follow a career in medicine. We had many things to be grateful for, and we wanted to express our gratitude to God by honoring him with a mass. She organized a small makeshift table for the priest. Then at night, we celebrated at my house dancing cumbia and salsa and talking deep into the night. My papa was very proud and happy that his oldest son was on his way to an American university.

"Education is the most powerful weapon which you can use to change the world."

—Nelson Mandela

20.
It's Okay to be Different

"What makes you unique, is what makes you strong."
—Harold Fernandez

As I glanced outside the arch-shaped window into the peace and serenity of the Hamilton Courtyard, I could not believe that this was all real. That, in fact, I was a student on this side of paradise, as Fitzgerald had detailed in the great American novel describing his existence at Princeton. My dormitory room in Hamilton Hall, which was part of Mathey College, seemed a magical sketch copied from a book of supernatural heroes and magnificent castles. Some nights, looking out the arch-shaped window of my dorm, I thought of imaginary characters and ghosts gliding through the air outside my room. The place was simply hypnotizing. Some afternoons I found myself staring for hours at the beauty of the spires and gargoyles, and the gothic columns and towers, and the trees and plants, and the perfectly manicured lawns outside my dormitory. It felt as if I was the main character in one of the books that I used to read with Mama on the green sofa. It was simply beyond reality. Often, I had to stop and convince myself that I was not dreaming, that I would not wake up and find myself in my tiny room in my apartment in West New York, or in my room at my house in Medellín agonizing with Mama about a thief breaking in. After admiring the beauty of this majestically designed courtyard, I turned to my roommate, Juan Almaguer, and said, "Juan, are you ready?"

He was sitting at his desk organizing some of the textbooks and notebooks that we had just bought at the university store. Classes were starting soon, and we had to be ready. I then said, "I think it's time to go, we have a meeting with our RA" My roommate was a Mexican- immigrant student from a poor high school in East Los Angeles, who had been a mathematics champion for the state of California. But Juan was a special young man. Despite having the physical appearance of a white Anglo-Saxon American, he had the soul and spirit of a humble Mexican-American immigrant. Joking around, I used to tell him sometimes, "Juan, you are more Mexican than any Mexican I have ever known." He was immensely proud of his heritage and culture. Moreover, he was also part of the legendary group of students in Los Angeles who had been trained by Jaime Escalante. This was the legendary teacher of mathematics who left a successful job in industry to teach calculus to a group of students in Los Angeles so that they could all pass the national mathematics achievement test. Juan not only passed the test, but he became a mathematics champion in California. After spending time with Juan, I would soon discoverer how immensely talented and intelligent he was.

Juan looked at me and said, "Yes, I am ready, let's go." We both went out of the room and walked down one set of stairs for our first meeting with the group of students in our dormitory as we were about to meet our residential advisor. A Mexican and an undocumented Colombian walking down the historical halls of the legendary Princeton University to meet fellow students. We went down one set of stairs and opened the door to his room and sat down by one of the corners of the living room as other students started to come and take their place. For some reason, I always preferred to sit in the corners or in the back of the room, always looking to keep a low profile so as not to be seen or heard. The real reason was that I was very nervous to be in this place and I felt uncomfortable in the presence of students that I thought were more qualified than me. After we were all there, the RA, an upper classman at Princeton, came in and introduced himself. That night he welcomed us to Princeton, and we went over guidelines and rules and all the resources that the university provided to help us in our education and different social activities. We also discussed, in detail, Princeton's "Honor Code," which he described as being "the rule of the land." Then he said, "I also want all of us to know a little about each other, so I want to ask you all to say a few words about where you come from, your family, and what your goals are here at Princeton."

Each student concisely spoke about their high schools, parents, and what they hoped to study at Princeton. Most of them had graduated from private academies or boarding schools, and their parents were doctors, lawyers, or owned large businesses. Then came my turn, and I could barely speak. My heart was racing, my hands were sweaty, and I was afraid that my voice would not come out. I was so nervous and conscious of my accent. In my mind I wondered, "What will they think of my accent? Will they think that I do not belong at Princeton?" By this time, I had made significant progress and felt more comfortable in the USA, but now at Princeton, I was concerned that other students might see me as inferior and think that I had been accepted to Princeton as an undeserving student for other reasons.

But I collected myself, and said in my heavy accent, "I am Harold Fernández, and my parents work in clothing and embroidery factories in New Jersey, and I am hoping to go to medical school after Princeton." I was often hesitant to share what my goals and objectives were. I thought that other students would make fun and think, "Who does he think he is? Why pretend that he will even become a doctor?" Then there was complete silence for a few seconds. I think they were waiting for me to elaborate on my hobbies or other interests. But I was done. I did not want to say anything else. Not by a malicious intent from other students, but because of my own internal fears and demons, I was intimidated by the accomplishments of the other students. One of them was the grandson of Nelson Rockefeller, and his home address was in Rockefeller Plaza in New York. I am sure that the students here didn't think much of the fact that my parents were not professionals, because I was now their classmate and I would be in the same classes with them and in the same activities. Nonetheless, there were many times that I felt inferior to them, and many times that I felt that they were better prepared than me because they went to better schools and they didn't have a heavy accent like I did. I was fortunate that Juan was my roommate and we had many things in common. We both were immigrants from poor families and, most importantly, we both had a heavy accent, spoke Spanish, and were passionate about soccer. Even more important, we both understood that our only way to get ahead in life was through a complete mastery of books.

As part of orientation, we had numerous small group meetings over the next few days, and after a while, I started to feel more comfortable sharing my story and revealing that my parents were factory workers. In fact, I started to feel proud of their jobs. I realized that although my parents did not have professional jobs, my parents' work was just as dignified and honest as the jobs of the parents of the other students there. Moreover, I had seen how hard my parents worked every day just to make ends meet and put food on the table. Each day, they used all their energy, enthusiasm, and passion to do the best possible work that they could. In fact, I began to embrace this as part of my own identity, and I felt emboldened and energized to follow their example and use the same amount of energy and passion that they had for their simple jobs in my education at Princeton. I would also think of Grandmother Alicia running her *arepa* business in Medellín and how she never took a day off, and Grandmother Rosa working every day despite having to go for her radiation therapy treatments. I realized that my parents did not have to be doctors, or lawyers, or famous, and that my love and respect for them and for all they had sacrificed to bring us to America was enough for me to feel proud of them, love them, and embrace their lives as the best example of perseverance in my own personal life. I began to feel a connection with them and to embrace this identity in my own path and struggle to become the best possible student that I could be.

As if the students and their backgrounds were not intimidating enough, everywhere I looked around Princeton, I found signs of its greatness, like pictures of Albert Einstein sitting in a lecture in Palmer Hall where I would be taking my physics class, or the building where George Washington had once slept during the Revolution. Nonetheless, in moments of inner reflection, I often felt like Amory Blaine, the protagonist in This Side of Paradise, as he walked "amongst the white funneled students." But at least Amory, although his mother was from the middle class, had been raised in the high points of society, reading all the classics by the time that he was a young teenager, and having been exposed to the classical music of Beethoven, Bach, and Mozart. I was definitely different. I had miraculously escaped the violence of my native Medellín, and then Memorial High School, where no student had ever been accepted to Princeton. My music had not been the classical symphonies of the great masters of the old world, but the songs and lyrics of Barrio Antioquia. Salsa from Puerto Rico and Cuba, vallenato from the coast of Colombia, and tango from Argentina. Songs like "El Preso" from Fruko y Sus Tesos that spoke about the agony and despair of being locked up in prison. Joe Arroyo's "Rebelion," which describes the suffering of African slaves as they arrive on the coast of Cartagena. "Virgen de las Mercedes," which talks about the patron saint of prisoners. And Hector Lavoe's "Calle Luna Calle Sol," which talks about the dangers of life in the barrio. These were the songs that I learned as a young boy on the corner just outside La Oasis. Lyrics that spoke to us about rebellion, African slaves, life in prison, despair, and suffering. This was the reality of my childhood, and now I found myself walking the narrow pathways of one of the greatest universities in the world.

I realized that my only chance to prove that I deserved to be a student here was by working hard. I had done well in high school. "How can I possibly do well at Princeton?" I often asked myself. I decided that I was going to make my dream of becoming a physician a reality. My first semester, I had a very tough schedule with physics, chemistry, and mathematics. I decided early on that I was not going to change my study routine. I thought that if it had worked so well at Memorial, where I faced so many challenges beyond academics, it would also serve me well at Princeton. I would continue to use the same energy, passion, enthusiasm, and mindset that I used to become the newspaper carrier of the month, to also do well at Princeton. The only thing that I changed was that over the next few weeks, I perfected my study routine. I designed a study routine that would then serve me well even into medical school and beyond. My new routine would require a space where I could just be alone with my books. I needed to find such a place at Princeton to put my plans into action.

"Everybody is a genius. But if you judge a fish by its ability to climb a tree, it will live its whole life believing that it is stupid."

—Albert Einstein

21.
Three Steps

"To really fall in love with books, you need to have your own strategy that works for you."
—Harold Fernandez

One night, as I made my way through the McCosh Hall Courtyard next to the university Chapel, I discovered one of the greatest gifts on this side of paradise. This building was truly special. In fact, this is the place where Einstein delivered the McCosh lecture for general relativity in 1921, the year before he received the Nobel Prize. I entered through one of the large wooden doors, went down one set of stairs, and walked through the labyrinth of narrow corridors until I found an empty classroom with a chalkboard. I made this room my own. I murmured to myself, "This is incredible. A gigantic room all for me to study at night. Wow!" Here, I discovered the peace and serenity of studying by myself without any distractions. Most students preferred to study in groups, some in Firestone Library. I often thought that this was too distracting.

Here in one of these classrooms was where I designed and perfected my studying strategy that I was going to use for my four years at Princeton. It consisted of three basic parts. First, I always tried to learn something about each subject before showing up for a lecture. The idea was not to become an expert or to know it all, but to quickly browse over the material so as to gain a superficial level of orientation when I showed up for the lecture. Second, I added a physical element to my study routine. I was never a student who could focus for a long period of time. I often found that my mind would start to wander, and I would become distracted by other thoughts or ideas. In addition, I discovered that sometimes, especially when studying mathematics or the hard-core sciences, I would drift into a deep sleep after trying to read for long periods of time. So what I started to do was to physically get up out of my seat and walk around the room for at least three to five minutes after reading one or two pages. My goal was never to read several pages in one sitting, it was only to read one or two pages at most, sometimes just a few paragraphs. As I walked around the room, I would recite aloud and try to repeat some of the concepts or ideas that I had just learned, and I would also visualize pictures and images of some of the things that I had just read. Then, after a few minutes, I would return to my seat and start reading again. The third, and probably most important, part was making an attempt to teach what I had just learned to someone else. I always felt that if you can teach it to someone else then it means that you really know it yourself. Initially, I didn't really have anyone that I could teach because everyone knew more than I did, so I would pretend that I was teaching a class of students. I would get up from my seat and walk over to the blackboard. I would get a piece of chalk, and in a loud voice I would pretend that I was teaching a class, and sometimes even pretend that students were asking me questions, and I would answer the questions. I found this system very effective and simple. It was very peculiar, and this was why I needed to be alone, and why I had to find a room for myself and why I could not study in the library with other students. There were many times when my close friends wondered about my whereabouts. I never divulged my secret hideout.

The big question now was, would this work here at Princeton? Would this method work in the most difficult class for premedical students at Princeton? I would soon find out because in no time, I found myself enrolled in organic chemistry with Dr. Maitland Jones. In student and academic circles, he was famous. I vividly remember the sight of students around campus wearing a T-shirt with the logo "I survived Jones." This was to showcase the pride felt by students who had taken his organic chemistry course and passed the test. There were some premedical students who knew how difficult this course was and would select not to take the course at Princeton, but to take it over the summer at another university because they were afraid that they might not do well. This was not an option for me. I had to take this course, and I had to meet this Professor Jones.

As I sat down in my seat in a classroom with over two hundred students eager to do their best in this course, I could not help but feel humble and grateful that I was there as a student. I thought to myself, "Wow, I am really here taking this course with the best students in America." There was no class at Princeton with a worse reputation and more history than organic chemistry with the legendary Professor Maitland Jones. We turned to him with laser focus, and the room was so quiet that you could hear the student next to you breathing. He walked up and down the stage holding a cup of tea, and in a very elegant fashion lit up a sequence of boards with chalk of different colors. Instead of appearing like an organic chemistry professor, he looked more like a classical painter waving his brush on a wide canvas, creating paintings that no one else had created before. Similarly, Dr. Jones moved his chalks of different colors, creating and drawing molecules on two dimensions in such a way as to describe their behavior with the environment and with each other in three dimensions. As Dr. Jones changed to a different colored chalk, the entire class of students would change the color of ink on their specially designed pens with a click, all in perfect synchrony. As he strode across the stage, he would take small brakes to pick up his cup of tea, take a sip, and then look into the audience of students.

After just a few minutes, I knew that this was a special man. In my view, Dr. Jones seemed more like a rock star than an organic chemistry professor. I was mesmerized by his personality, his method of teaching, and his charisma. It didn't matter at all that English was not my first language; I completely connected with him. I followed every single move that he made during his lessons. I copied with intensity and fervor every word that came out of his mouth. At the end of each class, my notebook was filled with drawings, lines, arrows, and gibberish that only I could comprehend. At the end of each lecture I would sprint to my room and, in peace at my desk, rewrite the entire lesson again but in neat and legible writing and supplementing each part with lessons from the textbook. In doing so, I compiled an entire beautiful, detailed set of all of Dr. Jones's lectures in a notebook that many other students would use years later.

I became a fanatic of organic chemistry. I lived, breathed, and dreamed organic chemistry. My dormitory's walls were adorned with molecules from his lessons. Everywhere I looked in my dormitory as I lay down to sleep each night, I would be reminded of problems or chemical reactions that we had discussed in class. I was consumed by organic chemistry.

One night late in the semester, I found that there was one concept that I did not understand well, and it was really upsetting me. I was having difficulty falling asleep. As I lay on my bed turning side to side, trying to fall asleep, I suddenly found a solution to the problem. I moved the blankets over to the side, got out of bed, and sat at my desk. I reached inside the drawer and took out my chemistry notebook to make the necessary corrections to solve the problem and find a solution. I then went back to bed and had no difficulty falling asleep. Without even realizing it, I had become fully immersed in this subject and I was loving it. As the semester progressed, I was enjoying the material so much that it didn't even feel as if I was working hard. I simply wanted to learn more and more, and to copy everything that Dr. Jones did.

Nonetheless, the final examination was soon approaching, and I would have the opportunity to show how well I understood the material.

The beauty and uniqueness of the Princeton mystery extended into all aspects of life, from its gothic buildings, to the grounds, to its peculiar professors, to even the way they administered examinations. For example, during the winter semester, final examinations are given to students at the end of January, after the Christmas break. This means that when students depart to rest and enjoy time with their families, they are not done with the semester because they have to come back to campus and take final examinations. There is no other major university in America that does this. Other students go home with the peace of mind that the semester is over, and they can therefore enjoy time with family and friends. But not at Princeton. So after having spent a few days with my family during the Christmas holidays, agonizing about the organic chemistry final, I returned to campus to study some more, and the day of the exam finally arrived.

On a cold winter night after having reviewed my notes all day, I finally decided that I was done studying for the final exam. I put all my notes down, took a brief shower, and then got ready to walk to Frick

Chemistry Laboratory for the final examination of my organic chemistry course. Because I had worked so hard, I felt confident that I would do well. But I also knew that Dr. Jones's final exams were as unconventional as his lectures. He didn't just give you simple questions with simple answers. In fact, we all expected that most of the questions would be about material that we had not even covered in class, and some of them didn't even have a known solution yet. He wasn't necessarily interested in a specific answer. He wanted to look inside our minds and find out if we understood the process and mechanisms of organic molecules to provide solutions to difficult problems. Each question was like a magical puzzle with many possible solutions. So there was also an element of uncertainty, which made me nervous. I was learning well and enjoying the class, but I also needed a good grade. I had a lot riding on my performance in this class. I wanted to be able to get into medical school.

As I approached Frick Laboratory, through the well-lit walkway behind the legendary Whig-Clio debate buildings, I began to see several other students coming from different directions on their way to take this final examination. It was around 7:30 p.m., and it was already dark outside. In the faces of my fellow students, I could also sense their nervousness and anxiety about this examination. We didn't know what to expect. We all slowly made our way inside, and I found a comfortable seat in the middle of a row. I liked this better so as not to be disturbed by other students walking in and out for other reasons. Soon after, a teaching assistant distributed the examination book, with the exam inside and instructions not to open it until 8 p.m. exactly. At the bottom of the front page was a place where we all had to sign and print our names. This was Princeton's Honor Code, and every student had to sign it prior to any examination. "I promise on my honor not to cheat, and also to turn in others who do." This is very serious at Princeton, as I would later find out. In fact, after the start of the exam, the professors leave, and they return later on to collect the completed examinations that are placed in the front of the room.

At exactly 8 p.m., Professor Jones, sitting on his desk at the front, said, "You may now start your exam, and make sure that you write down all your mechanisms of equations as you solve the problem. Best of luck." He then left, and the room became completely silent as we all started to read the examination and started working on the problems. As my hands trembled and I struggled to turn the first page of the booklet to read the first problem, I felt an immense sense of peace and comfort. It was not an easy problem, but I realized that I understood it, and I had a complete mastery of the advanced tools and understanding of organic molecules and processes to find a reasonable solution. I went ahead to the next problem and all the other pages, and I felt the same sense of peace with each one. We had about three hours to complete the exam, and I was done after about two hours. I spent another twenty minutes reviewing my answers and perfecting the equations. I then grabbed both the workbook and the examination booklet, walked over to the front desk, and placed each one on its respective pile. I then collected my pencils and put on my coat, and slowly made my way out of the room to meet with some of my friends. The test was so exhausting and so difficult that we all made an unconscious pact not to discuss the questions or answers afterwards. We just gathered a small group and walked together back to Mathey College, enjoying light conversation and delighting our eyes with the beauty of this magical campus and walkways.

In my mind, I would remind myself that this was real. "Yes, Harold, it is you," I said to myself, walking down through East Pyne and the historical alleys described in This Side of Paradise. And even more importantly, I was starting to feel that I belonged here, and that I could do well here despite my shortcomings with my accent and others matters related to my immigration status in America. It was close to midnight, and we all wanted to get some sleep before starting to prepare for the next final exam. When I got to my dormitory, I got ready for bed and lay down. I had no trouble falling asleep that night. I was content with the work that I had put into my class, and although the test had been difficult, I was confident that I would do well.

Actually, I did do very well on this test. I also did very well in all of my other courses. I realized, however, that I had done well not because I was more intelligent than my classmates, but because I worked very hard. And, even more importantly, because I had developed a system of reading and studying that worked for me. A few weeks later, I received a letter from the dean of students that said, "Dear Harold, after reviewing your grades, I am happy to inform you that your grades place you as one of the top students at the university." When I read this letter, I was shocked. I wanted to cry from the immense happiness that I felt. This was the time when I started to feel in my heart that I did belong at Princeton. I saved the letter in the top drawer of my desk, hidden but easily accessible each time that I had doubts about my abilities or whether I belonged here. Upon reading this letter, I honestly felt as if I was walking on clouds. My system of studying was working.

"Only the disciplined ones in life are free."
—Eliud Kipchoge

"If you don't like something, change it. If you can't change it, change your attitude."
—Maya Angelou

22.
A Solitary Walk

"You see, I viewed these books as my protection. These books were my escape into a different reality."
—Harold Fernandez

With each passing day, I was enjoying more and more my life on this side of paradise. Yet despite my academic triumphs and the affection that I was receiving from my new community of friends, I was as lonesome as any young man can ever be. I was trapped in my thoughts, and in my fears that I was only living in a dream that would soon end. I knew that I had a secret that no one else could know, not even my closest friends at Princeton, not even my sweet girlfriend Tina. Heavily immersed in my schoolwork, accompanied by some of the most intelligent young people in the world in the greatest academic environment, I was carrying a heavy burden in my heart.

I was terrified of what the next day would bring. All night I prayed on my bed, staring at the ceiling, unable to close my eyes and get some sleep. God knows that I needed some rest since I had been studying like a lunatic so that I could do well in my courses. Every night I was going to sleep past midnight and waking up early to start the routine of reading my books early.

For several days, I had been preoccupied thinking about the appointment that my family had with the immigration judge in the Newark office. I had not told anyone about this deep secret that I had. My mind was paralyzed by fear. As I lay down on my bed in my dorm room, trying to fall asleep, I just kept wondering about what would happen the next day when we all faced our immigration judge. Would he act with compassion and stamp our passports with "suspension of deportation procedures," as he had previously done, or would he simply take away all of our rights and place all of us in detention in preparation of deportation. This was the big unknown each time that we faced the immigration judge at these hearings. I had taken to bed early so that I could get an early start in the morning, but I just couldn't close my eyes and get good sleep.

I woke up very early. Looking out my window, I could tell that it was still dark outside. Because Juan was so tall, we agreed from the start of the year that he would get the bunk bed at the bottom. I had the top. When my watch hit 5 a.m., I turned carefully so as not to disturb Juan, climbed down, collected my small bag with toiletries, opened the door, and went downstairs to the basement to take a shower. When I returned, Juan was still sleeping, so I carefully got dressed and picked up my bag with several of my books. The night before, I had prepared it with my calculus, chemistry, and physics textbooks. I was taking a pre-med curriculum, and these were the courses that I had. I walked out of the room and closed the door behind me. As I made my way down the Hamilton yard and then through the majestic Palmer Arch and down the stairs, I realized that the campus felt very lonely. Many of the students were still sleeping and had not gotten up for their classes yet. As I made my way down through the graduate housing dorms toward the dingy train station, I felt an immense sense of solitude. No one in the university actually knew where I was going. What if I didn't return? What would be the news if the immigration judge ordered for all of us to be kept in custody and deported back to our native country? As I made this lonely walk, I tried to put all these fears away and concentrate on absorbing the beauty of this astonishing university. I glanced at the beautiful gothic buildings, adorned with large stained-glass windows and arches and small walkways and halls connecting separate parts of the buildings. These dorms had seen many important people through the centuries: Albert Einstein, Woodrow Wilson, John F. Kennedy, F. Scott Fitzgerald, and many others. As I made my way from the upper part of the campus toward the dingy station, I walked through some of the dormitories that housed the upperclassmen, including Spellman Hall. They were actually small apartments with their own living rooms and kitchens so that students could cook their own meals. I thought that this was so cool, and I wondered if I would get the opportunity to one day live in these dormitories.

As I strolled down these paths, I did feel an immense sense of gratitude for everything that I had experienced so far. In a way, I was content that even if it was for a fleeting moment, I was part of paradise. With this thought came a sense of belonging. I then quickly realized that in fact I also had a great responsibility, and that was to do well as a student. Therefore, I quickly drifted again to thinking about my books. For a moment I thought that I hadn't brought enough of them. You see, I viewed these books as my protection. These books were my escape into a different reality. I searched the pages of these books desperately, seeking all information that I could find, knowing that mastering this information would make me a great doctor.

I got on the train, which took me to Princeton Junction, and then switched trains to Newark. From there I would simply walk to the immigration center on Main Street. There I met my family. They were all there already waiting in the line outside the building. We were usually there very early because we realized that this would get us in quicker. We were all there: my father, mother, and Byron, and my two younger American brothers, Marlon and Alex. All of us were dressed up neatly as if we were going to a special baptism celebration. We knew that it was important to appear decent in the eyes of the judge, so we all dressed up. In a single line, we would then make our way into the immigration building and proceed to the large room to wait for the doors to open. As I looked around, I could see that there were hundreds of immigrant families from all different corners of the world waiting to meet their fate in front of the judge.

At 8 a.m., the door promptly opened, and we all moved in past the checkpoint and quickly grabbed a number and moved inside the big room to wait until our number got called. The room filled quickly. As we waited, I studied. My mother would prompt me to take a break and relax, but I knew that I had to use this time effectively. This was also a way for me to deal with my fears of what could happen if the judge ordered our immediate deportation. I had to open up my backpack and take out books to read. Other people around me thought that I was a weirdo reading these heavy books of physics, biology, and chemistry. The tension in this room was palpable. The eyes around me were those of immigrant children and families hoping to fix their problems so that they could become American citizens. Each family with their own hopes and dreams. You could see it in their eyes. Many families with their children from all different parts of the world. All of us with the same dream to be accepted into this wonderful country as legal residents so that we could officially come out of the shadows and dream of a better future.

I had a more immediate need. As we found a place to sit, I turned to my mother and said, "Mama, I will be sitting in that corner reading, please let me know when we are called." I had something to do. I had a lot of work, and I didn't want to get behind. As we waited and the hours passed, I found a great escape in my books that I would take out one by one. First chemistry, then biology, and then physics. Within all the noise and the sense of tension, I found a sense of peace and solace as I read each book and realized that I was taking small steps to make myself a better person and eventually a better doctor. Periodically, I would look up at my parents anxiously waiting and praying in silence that things would go well.

After a few hours of waiting, we finally heard our number being called over the intercom. In one single motion, we all jumped out of our seats and made our way toward the courtroom. There we met our lawyer, who reviewed our information with us and then instructed us to sit in the front row together so that the judge could see us. He wanted to make sure that the judge understood that he was deciding the fate of an entire family, including our youngest members, Alex and Marlon, who were born on American soil. In addition, our lawyer had other documents showing that both of my parents were hard workers, paid taxes, and had immaculate records in America. My parents' police report was so clear that they didn't even have traffic violations. He also had information showing that both Byron and I had been Scouts and that I was an Eagle Scout, had been valedictorian of my high school, and was now a student at Princeton University.

After we waited for a few minutes, the court clerk called everyone to attention and announced that the judge would be entering. The judge then walked in, sat on his chair, and took a few minutes to review some paperwork on his desk. He then called for our case, and our lawyer approached the bench. They went over a few papers. He then asked for our passports and put a stamp on them and gave them back to our lawyer. He then called for the next case. We quietly moved over to the side and followed our lawyer out of the room. We were petrified because we did not know what he had stamped on the passports. We rushed to our lawyer and he said, "Stay calm, everything is all right." The judge had once again stamped "suspension of deportation procedures" on our passports. We all took a deep breath and smiled. This was all we wanted. This meant that we could still stay in America. The judge realized that we did not meet any of the legal categories to grant us a green card, but he also did not feel that it was humane to deport a family like this, in part because this would have been detrimental to my two youngest brothers, who were American citizens.

We smiled and hugged one another with a sigh of relief. Mama said, "Thank you, Lord, for giving us more time in America." I gathered all my belongings and accompanied my family out of the immigration building. Although we had not gotten our green cards, we were all very happy not to be deported. This was the one possibility that we all feared. This was the possibility that all the immigrants in that building going in front of the judge feared. We were lucky. We could enjoy our time until our next meeting with the judge in about six to twelve months. We exited the building together and said our goodbyes outside. My family would then return to the apartment in West New York, and I would go back to the train station to get the train that would bring me to Princeton Junction and back to my paradise.

That night, after returning to campus from my small secret journey to the immigration courts, I felt a sense of peace inside of me. I realized that I had more time. After dinner at Hamilton Hall, I made my way to my secret hideaway in the basement of McCosh Hall to continue with my studies. As I laid my books on the table and started my study routine, I was distracted by thoughts of coming up with other things that I could possibly do to improve our chances with the immigration judge. I then came up with the idea of writing letters to President Reagan and to prominent Princeton alumni. So I drafted letters to our Republican president, Ronald Reagan, and to the governor of New Jersey, Thomas Kean, and to the senator of New Jersey, Bill Bradley. Both the governor and the senator were Princeton alumni. Bill Bradley was also the famous Rhodes Scholar, NCAA star, and leader of the national champions Nicks team who was quickly becoming a national political star.

In the letter, I introduced myself and my background, and I explained that I was a student at Princeton but did not have legal documents. I also described how I wanted to one day be able to go to medical school and help people through medicine. I asked them to please send me a letter of support that I could then show to our judge the next time that we had a trial. The next day I sent out all the letters in the mail. A few months later, I received letters of support from all of them. I made copies and sent them to our lawyer. I wanted to make sure that we were even better prepared for our next trial. I wanted to do everything that I could possibly do to increase my chances. I also wanted to ask officials at Princeton to give me letters of support, but then I realized that I could not do this because the university did not know my real immigration status. They thought that I was a legal resident because this was what I had checked on my initial application. I felt better having received these letters of support that I could have in my file, but every night I remained with the intense feelings of being an impostor because I could not tell Princeton about my legal status. This was about to change.

"You can't speed up the river and you can't slow it down; at a certain point you got to have some faith.

—Inky Johnson

23.
A Second Chance

"It's okay to cry. In fact, at some point, we all may need to cry."
—Harold Fernandez

As spring descends on the Princeton campus, the flowers begin to bloom, the grass becomes greener, and the entire place comes alive with renewed energy. As early as March, many classes would begin to meet outside on the perfectly manicured lawns outside McCosh Hall. On sunny days, many students would lie on the grass wearing little clothing, trying to advance the color of their skin to a tanner complexion. In the afternoons before dinner, other students would participate in outdoor activities such as playing Frisbee, having picnics, and enjoying outdoor parties. The energy of the other students was contagious.

I felt stronger and more self-assured at this point than I had at any other time. Instead of being distracted by the pleasant surroundings, I was strengthened to concentrate and work even harder. Although I was participating in some of the social and leisurely activities, most of my time was still spent with my books. The coursework was more difficult, but I was gaining confidence with each passing day. Everything appeared too perfect; I was sure something was about to change. I was correct, for one of my old secrets would come back to haunt me.

The progress that I had made toward feeling like a legitimate part of this legendary community screeched to an abrupt halt one spring evening during my second semester. The academic year was going fast. We would soon be going home for the spring holiday and then returning for a month-long reading period that would be followed by final exams. I was eagerly looking forward to going home, to tasting my mother's Colombian cooking again and listening to Colombian Cumbia. I followed my usual midweek routine. I had dinner with my friends at the Hamilton dining hall and then returned to my dorm room. On the ground floor I headed, as usual, toward the mailbox. There was a letter. I noticed that it was from the university's dean of foreign students, Janina Issawi. I assumed that it was an invitation to a social event for foreign students stuck at Princeton during the holiday break. I tore the envelope open and read the letter. I was wrong. This was not an invitation to any celebration; this was a serious letter. It was an official letter reminding foreign-born students who were not yet American citizens to set up an appointment with Mrs. Issawi and bring along their original legal residency documents so that they could be photocopied for inclusion in the student's file. The letter further explained that this was an official request to allow the federal government to keep track of students who were permanent residents and who were receiving government grants or loans, as I was. But this letter was not a routine matter for me. Princeton had already seen a copy of my green card in my application for admission, but now the dean needed to see the original, and I knew that the original was a forgery purchased by my parents on the black market. Walking into a Princeton dean's office and handing her a fake document would not be routine for me.

The abysmal hole in my stomach was the polar opposite of the joy I had felt when I had received the letter from Dean Kanach congratulating me on my first semester grades. It was as if everything had been instantly overturned. I said to myself, "Oh my God, my Princeton career is about to end." The dream of American success that had begun at an abandoned dock on the Florida coast was about to shatter.

For the next few days, I was consumed with figuring out what I should do. I did not speak about the dean's request with my parents. I knew that it would tear them apart to learn that I might be expelled, that I might be barred from the American opportunities they had worked so hard to give me. They were so proud that I was a student at Princeton. I pictured my father's locker at work, plastered with newspaper articles—in English and Spanish—about my accomplishments in the classroom and on the field. He would often call his friends, bosses, or even random visitors and show them the inside of his locker. His boss might earn more money, have a more prestigious job, but he did not have a son at Princeton.

As I lay on my bed during those dreadful nights, I would think of how terrible it would be for my parents, how much they would cry, if I were to suddenly arrive at our apartment in West New York—luggage in hand—and tell them, "It is over—my career at Princeton is finished." I am not exaggerating when I say that my parents would have died of sorrow.

My choices were simple. I could meet with the dean and show her my fake green card and hope she might not notice. Or I could confess and tell her that I did not have any legal documents. I no longer had the heart for the first option. It was pure fear. I remembered how, a few years earlier, I had failed to follow all the way through with my plan to get a social security card in Long Branch, New Jersey. If a government clerk could frighten me so, how much more was I frightened by the prospect of having to fool a Princeton dean? So I wanted to confess my actions to someone I could trust.

Over the course of the semester, I had come to feel that my professor in Spanish literature, Arcadio Díaz-Quiñones, was not only a foremost scholar, but also a kind, wise, and generous friend. So, a few days after I had opened the dean's letter, I waited after his class and asked if he could spare a few minutes. He put me at ease by telling me I could have as much time as I wanted. He closed the door, and we sat down next to each other at the end of the long rectangular table.

As I was about to speak, I sensed that I would not utter a single word without breaking down. The tension and anxiety that had built up inside of me exploded. Before I said any words, I dropped my head on the table and wept. Professor Díaz put his hand on my shoulder and held it there consolingly. After a few minutes, I collected myself and described all that I had done to get into this country and my efforts ever since to disguise my residency status. I told him how frightened I was that I would be expelled from Princeton and what that would do to my family.

Professor Díaz listened patiently. He was interested in every detail of my story, almost as if he were intently reading some vivid, picturesque novel. When I was done, he advised me not to tell anyone else about what had happened and to keep plugging along with my schoolwork. He assured me that he would speak to Mrs. Issawi, who was a close friend. He also said that he would discuss the problem with the dean of students, Eugene Lowe, and the president of the university, William G. Bowen. The thought that such authority figures would be analyzing my case terrified me, but Professor Díaz's confidence seemed to calm me down.

Soon after our conversation, Professor Díaz discussed my case with President Bowen. Professor Díaz was hopeful that the president would see my case with compassion because of his long history at Princeton of making decisions that greatly increased the diversity of the student body, such as opening its doors to women in 1969, and to more African-American students and Jewish students in the 1970s and 1980s. Now, for the first time, he would have to decide the fate of an undocumented student in his beautiful university.

President Bowen did not hesitate to decide. That evening, President Bowen returned a call to Professor Díaz at his own home and told him that he had reached a conclusion on my case after a discussion with various academic deans. Without hesitation and in the firmest way, he informed professor Díaz that he had decided that I could remain as a student at Princeton University. Filled with emotion and with tears in his eyes, Professor Díaz said, "Thank you, Bill, you are a great man. God will reward you for your generosity and compassion. You have just made the greatest gift to this young man." But before my pardon was official, there were a few things that I had to do. The first one was to meet with the dean of my college, Nancy Weiss. As we met in her office, I found Mrs. Weiss to be compassionate. I felt at ease in her presence, although I feared what she might say. She started by saying that Princeton was proud to have me in its student body. Nevertheless, she described two formidable issues that the university now had to confront. First, I had broken the students' honor code. This essential Princeton tradition affirms that you cannot cheat or lie, and I had lied. Then, she said, I had been receiving government grants intended for American citizens or permanent residents. Since I was neither, my taking the money violated the law. "But,

Harold," she said, "both problems have solutions, and President Bowen and the university want to help you."

Just as I was feeling crushed by the gravity of my situation, Mrs. Weiss gave me a glimmer of hope. I looked up with an invigorated concentration. To address the first issue, she said, I would have to write a substantial essay explaining my understanding of the school's honor code, how I had broken it, and why I wanted a pardon. To resolve the second problem, Princeton would change my status to that of a foreign student. With that change, the university would furnish all my grants and loans with its own funds, not with those of the federal government. This change meant that Princeton would be contributing a significant amount of money so that I could study there. It was like having a full Princeton scholarship.

As I exited Mrs. Weiss's office, I wanted to yell and jump up and down with happiness. I felt as if I was walking on clouds. I felt so grateful toward Princeton. I murmured as I walked into the courtyard, "Oh my Lord, thank you for this gift. Thank you for giving me this opportunity so that I can stay here at Princeton."

For several weeks, I did not share with my parents the details of how Princeton discovered my undocumented status. I realized that this would have been devastating for them, and I waited until most of the issues had been resolved. Then, I traveled home for a weekend and explained to them what had happened—but in reverse order. I told them that everything had been solved, that Princeton had arranged for us to meet with one of its lawyers that specializes in immigration, and that he would be trying to help us. Then I explained how Princeton came to put us in touch with its lawyer, and about my confession. As I told them the story, my mother sat next to me, gently weeping. She felt terrible that their decision to enter the country without documents had put me through such anguish and that they had been able to do little to help.

Mama said, "Harold, my love, you are a great young man. Keep working hard, and your dreams will become a reality." Papa had been silent, fearing the worst, and he finally said, "Oh, my son, please forgive us for having put you through such torment, but keep working hard and America will keep on helping you."

A few days later, I received a second letter from Senator Bradley.

When I looked at the envelope and saw that it was an official letter from his office, I had a difficult time understanding the reason for a second letter. I asked myself, "Why is the senator writing again if he already sent me a letter of support that I could show the judge?" I finally opened the envelope and read the letter. Briefly, he wanted to know who was the judge that would handle our case in immigration and when our next trial was. He asked me to call his office and give this information to his assistant. I was stunned when I read this. "What an incredible man our senator is," I thought. He is spending effort on helping a student who cannot even vote. A few days later, I finally got the courage and called his office. I spoke to his assistant and gave her the information that she had requested. She was very pleasant over the phone, and I got the feeling that she had been waiting for my call from the brief conversation that I had with her.

That night I went to sleep under a blanket of questions and fears that I could not evade. I was relieved that I had finally confessed my secret to Princeton and that I was pardoned and allowed to remain there as a student. However, the reality was that I was still an undocumented immigrant and I would soon be facing the immigration judge again. As I lay down on my bed, I wondered if the letters that I had obtained from President Reagan, Governor Kean, and Senator Bradley would make a difference. I wondered if Senator Bradley had actually reached out to the immigration judge and if his attempts would help me and my family obtain our permanent residency. I had so many questions. I had so many fears that I was at the edge of getting deported along with my family. I had so many fears that I would have to leave my wonderful existence on this side of paradise.

"You must love your neighbor as yourself."
—Jesus

24.
Peace of Mind

"I was beginning to see that all my successes in America and my triumphs in my classes were directly related to my love for books."
—Harold Fernandez

The day that I had been dreading finally arrived. We had our next visit with the immigration judge early in the morning. Once again, I went through my preparation ritual just as I had done a few months before. First and foremost, I prepared my bag with my books. This was the most important part of the ritual. These books were my escape outside the worries and the fears that filled my soul as I thought about the possibility of getting deported and having to abandon Princeton. Each time that I sensed my thoughts and imagination drifting into pessimism, I would simply open one of my books and hide my thoughts in its pages. In an instant, I would be transported into another reality that was much more comfortable and rewarding. This was the world of Princeton academia and the world of scientific discovery and biological and physical processes that I had been learning about from some of the most remarkable professors in the world. I went to bed early, and before closing my eyes, sent a prayer to our Lord in the way that my grandmothers had taught me, to protect us and to enlighten the judge with humanity and compassion as he was deciding the fate of my family.

The next day, I traveled to Newark and met my family at the immigration building. After going through the same frightening routine of waiting in long lines and overfilled rooms, we soon found ourselves standing in front of the immigration judge. Prior to this, I had implored our lawyer to make sure that he specifically showed the judge all the letters that we had obtained from government officials and also from several of the academic deans at Princeton. He promised me that he would.

Soon after opening the court, the judge called our family. Our lawyer approached the bench, and they had a brief conversation. From where I was standing, I could see the judge looking intently at each document in our file, reading each one through his reading glasses, and going back and forth. Intermittently, he would raise up his head and look at us. My parents had their heads down, while I was standing upright looking straight at him, almost making eye contact each time that he raised his head. I was trying in my mind to make a connection with him and ask for compassion. After a few minutes, he called our lawyer again and asked him a few more questions. Then suddenly he called us to the front and asked for our passports. He passed them to the clerk, who proceeded to put stamps on them. He then looked at us and said, "Welcome to the United States." Just like that, he decided to grant me and my entire family legal permanent residency in the most beautiful country in the world. We were all in a state of shock. Motionless, speechless, we all wanted to go up and hug this judge and express our gratitude for making this decision that would allow us to continue living in America. With one decision, he completely changed our lives. We went from living in the shadows and hiding from the immigration service to legal permanent residents.

This was obviously one of the most important moments of my life, and I honestly did not know how to react. The possibility of getting a green card at this trial was the furthest thing from my mind. We had heard from all the lawyers and the experts that getting legal residency is very complicated and that it would eventually require that we leave the country, request a visa in a consulate in our native country, and then return legally into the United States. I was thrilled to hear this would not be necessary.

We then exited the courtroom as the judge called the name of another family. Outside the courtroom, we gathered with our lawyer and he explained what had happened. I interpreted this to my parents. Both of them were crying from happiness. My papa was in complete disbelief.

"This is not possible. I can't believe this. I know we must leave before we get our residency." Papa was so incredulous that he told us, "We must not believe this until we actually get our residency cards in the mail." Our lawyer then explained that this was real. He said, "Through a miracle, the judge has granted your family legal permanent residency. You are all now legal residents of the United States. You can apply for United States citizenship in five years, and in a few months, you will get your cards in the mail." My mama could not hide her excitement. This was her dream come true. Every night for the last ten years, she had been praying for the day that we were legal residents. Her eyes and her face were filled with pure joy. "Oh my Lord, thank you for hearing my prayers, dear God." We then gathered as a family, hugged one another with intense passion and happiness, and together accompanied my mother in expressing our gratitude for this special gift from God.

After the celebrations, I made my way back to the train station so that I could return to my beloved Princeton. But it was different now. In the early morning before the sun was out, I had left my paradise as an undocumented immigrant, and now I was returning as a completely legal resident. As I walked around campus that night, I was a new person. The heavy emotional burden of not having documents and feeling like an imposter within my own school was now lifted from my shoulders. I felt light. I felt strong. I felt that the sky was the limit and I was now free to concentrate on my books and become even more passionate about my studies without the fear and despair that so often accompanied me on my strolls around campus or late into the nights as I tried to get some rest.

With my newfound mental and emotional freedom and peace of mind, I soon discovered an enormous passion and love for the slowly developing field of molecular biology. One afternoon, during one of our laboratory sessions in a biology course, we made some simple experiments with the chemical substance in every one of our cells that provides the instructions of life. In scientific terms, this chemical substance is called DNA, but in simple terms, this is the material found in the nucleus of our cells that provides the instructions for every single activity that occurs in our cells and therefore in our bodies. The experiment was simple. It involved purifying a sample of DNA in a small test tube, cutting it into pieces with enzymes specifically designed to target the piece of DNA at specific sites, separating the different fragments by running them on a gelatin surface exposed to an electrical current at either end to separate them according to their size, and then processing the gelatin to see where the different bands were found. When I saw the photograph of the gel for the first time, I whispered to myself, "This is the coolest thing that I have ever seen." This concept that one could actually work with DNA, manipulate it, cut it, and make it do things in bacteria (like insulin for example) was just mesmerizing.

In addition, recently there had been a lot of work on a new gene. Scientists had isolated and identified the piece of DNA that is responsible for the debilitating condition called cystic fibrosis. This is a terrible condition that affects young people, and it interferes with a passage in the membrane of their cells causing the secretions in their lungs and in their stomach to be very thick and not work properly. There is no cure for this condition. The young people afflicted with this disease die in their second or third decade of life from pulmonary complications. But upon identifying the gene and the mutation responsible for the disease, there was a lot of hope that by using molecular biology, we could cure it; the genetic defect was very simple since it only involved one base pair, which leads to a change in one amino acid. At this time, this was the simplest genetic defect ever discovered, and there was a lot of hope and enthusiasm that soon we would be able to find a cure for this condition by altering this genetic defect.

I got caught up in this excitement. I wanted to be involved in this research. I decided that I would major in molecular biology at Princeton, and I therefore became a fanatic of this new field. I quickly signed up in the department. I found a laboratory where I could train and help out with one of the new rising stars of the department, Dr. Jean Schwarzbauer. I soon became immersed in this field with the same passion and energy that I had used as a young immigrant to become the best newspaper boy in America. I now wanted to become the best molecular biologist in America. I decorated my room with the magic of molecular biology. I covered the walls, the ceilings, every single corner with posters and drawings of the different molecules of DNA. Each night I went to bed thinking and dreaming of molecular biology.

Over the next few years, I would immerse myself in all areas of molecular biology, first learning all the basic concepts of chemistry, organic chemistry, and biochemistry and then mastering the more complex areas of research and laboratory experiments in molecular biology. As a young student, I found Princeton a haven for research, discovery, and innovation in this new field. I had the incredible opportunity to do important work, even as a young undergraduate student.

Dr. Jean Schwarzbauer concentrated her efforts on understanding how a protein called fibronectin behaved. This protein would now become my best friend. This is a protein that penetrates the cell membrane or its outer covering. In doing so, it was believed that this protein had an important role in communication between the interior of the cell and its surroundings. Moreover, there was some evidence that this protein was important in how cells move around, especially how defective cells can move into the blood circulation. Even more important, she had a hypothesis that this protein might be an important mediator of how cancer cells migrate from one part of the body into other parts, causing cancer. My specific role was to find out the chemical sequence of bases of DNA pairs in a specific fragment of the DNA molecule that coded for the fibronectin gene, and then use computer analysis of the sequence to see if we could figure out how this protein was involved in cancer formation. This was in fact my thesis project at Princeton University.

I became passionate about this project and spent many days and nights, weekends, and also the entire summer after my junior year advancing this research. I dreamed every night that I could somehow contribute even a small granule of sand to the mountain of research that would need to be done to find a cure for this terrible disease that had caused so much pain and suffering to Grandmother Rosa. I was living my dream. I was doing important work that could one day be used to help people with cancer.

One night as I was going to sleep, surrounded by what appeared to be a museum to DNA, I reflected on where my secret journey to America had brought me. With a smile on my face, I recalled the colorful picture books that I would read with my mama on the green sofa when I was just beginning to mouth words under the most caring guidance and love that any child can receive. In my dormitory and my rooms where I would study in the confines of the four walls that surrounded me, I would often reminisce about the ever-fearful violence and increasing danger in the streets of Barrio Antioquia that I was fortunate to leave behind. Now, immersed in the magic of the Princeton campus, I was falling asleep, reading my complex research papers and textbooks of molecular biology in perhaps the greatest university in the world. I often remembered Mama's words: "Books will change your life." I was starting to understand what my mama was saying. I was beginning to see that all my successes in America and my triumphs in my classes were directly related to my love for books.

"No matter who you are or what you look like, how you started off, or how and who you love, America is a place where you can write your own destiny."

—Barak Obama

25.
Giving Back

"Never underestimate the pure joy of helping your parents."
—Harold Fernandez

One early afternoon in January of my senior year, as I made my way from a modern art seminar at McCosh Hall to my dormitory in Patton Hall, I stopped a few times to breathe in the fresh air of Princeton's gardens and also to appreciate some of the fine architectural details and statues that adorn the many historic buildings of this beautiful campus. I was deeply aware that I would soon be moving on to another place. I was looking forward to other challenges, but my heart was filled with nostalgia at the thought of leaving a place that had given me so much. But there was one more final gigantic surprise.

On my way to my room, I saw a couple of friends who informed me that the dean's office was looking for me. Initially, I didn't think too hard about this. But then as I was entering my dormitory, another friend also said, "Hey, Harold, the dean's office wants to speak with you. They said to go by their office today." I replied, "Thanks, I'll drop my books in my room and I will walk over to the office."

I opened the door to my room and noticed the red flashing lights on the deck of my answering machine indicating that there were a few messages there. I leaned over, pressed the message button, and the first message was from the dean's office. "Harold, this is Dr. Eugene Lowe's office. When you hear this message, please come to our office on the second floor of West College as soon as possible." When I heard this message, I was alarmed that something was wrong. My head was spinning in a thousand directions. I asked myself, "Oh my God, what did I do? Am I in some kind of trouble? Why so much urgency? Why do they want to see me right away?" In my mind, I was already thinking of the worst possible scenarios. I thought that something terrible must have occurred. As I rushed to drop off my books on my desk and change into a more formal shirt to go and meet with Dean Lowe, my hands were trembling, my heart was racing, my thoughts were cloudy. I was asking myself, "Oh God, is this related to my immigration problems from the past? Am I getting expelled from school? What did I do wrong?" In all the confusion, I managed to change my shirt and rush out of my room, down the stairs, and to the main road that leads to the path to West College, which is just about five minutes away. This was a very short distance, but it felt like the longest walk of my life.

I opened the door to West College and rushed up one set of stairs to find Dean Lowe's office. I felt my heart racing and my head spinning as I made my way up the stairs. As I walked inside to meet the secretary, I tried as hard as I could to regain my composure. I then came inside and said, "Hi, my name is Harold Fernández. I am a student in the class of '89, and I received a call to come and see Dean Lowe." The secretary then looked at me and with a big smile, her eyes full of joy, said in an enthusiastic voice, "Oh my Lord, Harold, we have been looking for you all day. Dean Lowe has to speak with you about something very important. He will be very happy to know that you are here. Please, take a seat right outside. Get a glass of water if you like, and he will be with you in a few moments." I responded, "Thank you, I will be right here waiting."

I stepped outside and took a seat. I was not in the mood for a glass of water. I was too nervous, although I was somewhat relieved by the pleasant tone and the smile of Dean Lowe's secretary. In my mind, it seemed very reassuring. I waited here for just a few minutes, which felt like an eternity. This evoked memories of waiting outside the office of the principal at Public School Number One in West New York during my first day of school in America. I vividly recalled the feelings of anxiety, fear, and uncertainty as I heard the sounds in English coming out of the intercom system in the hall. As a recent immigrant who had gone through so much to get my legal documents, I couldn't stop thinking that something had gone terribly wrong with my previous immigration woes.

Then I saw Dean Lowe open the door himself and with a pleasant smile say, "Harold, it is so nice to see you. Please come inside my office so we can talk." As I approached him, he gave me a strong handshake and put his right arm around my shoulder and said, "Come on in, Harold, we have great news for you." I went inside and sat in front of his desk as he gave some instructions to his secretary, and then came inside and closed the door behind him. He then sat down, took a sip of water, crossed his legs on his chair, and started to describe the history and the selection process for the most prestigious prize that is given to an undergraduate student at Princeton. This is the Moses Taylor Pyne Honor Prize. I actually was very aware of this prize, and honestly, I think that most students at Princeton know the significance of this award. He leaned over his desk, and with a smile he said, "You see, Harold, this is a prize that has been around this institution for over a hundred years, and you have been selected as one of the recipients this year. Please accept my most sincere congratulations. I know how hard you have worked, and I am happy that you have been selected." He paused for a brief moment, looked around his office, and said, "I know you must be in shock right now, and I apologize for the sudden news, but this is a prize that the university takes very seriously, and it is done with the utmost secrecy using a selection process that involves many interviews with different people around the entire university, including professors, coaches, administrators, and other staff. The prize is given at an official ceremony on alumni day in February at the legendary Jadwin Gym, and it also comes with a monetary award."

I knew exactly what this prize was. Every student at Princeton knows what the "Pyne" prize is because it is the most prestigious award given to a graduating student. I was shocked beyond words. In my mind, I tried to search for something to say. I had rushed to see the dean thinking that I was in some sort of trouble related to my history as an undocumented student, and I was now receiving the biggest news of my life. This magnificent university was recognizing my hard work and my sacrifice and my commitment to books and academia. The only thing that I mustered to say was, "Thank you, Dean Lowe, thank you from the bottom of my heart. This recognition means the world to me, and I am so grateful that I have been given this opportunity to be a student here." I reached over and shook his hand. As I turned to leave the office, he said, "My secretary will be in contact with you to make plans for the press conference to make the announcements tonight, and then for the awards ceremony during alumni day. Now you can go on and tell all your friends."

After I was out of West College, I regained my composure and started running toward my dormitory. I was so happy. I had to tell somebody. I had to share this with my friends. Once in my room, I found Juan was already there, and I said, "Juan, you are not going to believe this. I cannot believe it myself, Juan. I have been awarded the Pyne prize." Juan rushed over to me and gave me a tight embrace, and said, "Great job, Harold. That is great news. You have worked so hard and you deserve this. I am so proud." All my friends were ecstatic and erupted into different expressions of happiness upon hearing the news. In an expression of humor, within my close circle of friends, they would refer to me as "Mr. Pyne." This was a big honor, and I was so proud and happy to be recognized, especially since just a few years before I was almost expelled from the university. Many notable alumni have won this prize, but the most distinguished one was actually a Latina student. This was the honorable Sonia Sotomayor, who had received the prize in 1975, and who would later go on to become one of the supreme court justices for our beloved country.

Alumni day finally arrived. I was anxious about having to address the large crowd of people and receiving my award. This is definitely one of the biggest celebrations on campus for alumni. Thousands of alumni return to campus. It is held every year, and during the main ceremony, which is held at Jadwin Gym, the university confers special prizes. One to an undergraduate alumnus for his work in the nation's service, another prize to a graduate student, and the third prize is the Moses Taylor Pyne Honor Prize to an undergraduate student as the highest general award given to a graduating senior. The entire gym is beautifully dressed up in the orange and black colors. Thousands of alumni wear traditional Princeton attire from their respective classes or wear bright ties, jackets, pants, and dresses with the school colors. The school spirit is palpable as alumni, their wives or husbands, and family celebrate the incredible honor of being part of this historic place.

As the ceremony was taking place, I was sitting with my parents at the main table right next to the stage. My parents were in awe, absorbing the energy and watching with great focus as the celebration unfolded. I had also invited Professor Díaz and his wife because they had become a special part of my life. President Bowen had just retired the year before, and therefore I would be getting the award from the new president, Dr. Harold Shapiro, the first Jewish president of Princeton.

I felt so much energy absorbing the celebration, but I just couldn't shake away the anxiety at the thought that I would have to go up on this stage and address so many important people. I had prepared a two-minute speech where I put my heart and soul in an honest expression of humility and gratitude toward my parents, my professors, and Princeton. Then my name was announced as one of the winners, and I was asked to come up to the stage. I looked at my humble mama and papa, held their hands for a second, gave my mama a kiss on her right cheek, and with renewed energy I climbed the five steps to the stage and approached Dr. Shapiro. He proceeded to introduce me and award me the prize, along with a white envelope with a check equivalent to half a year's tuition at Princeton. Susanne Hagedorn, my co-recipient, had just received her prize and had addressed the crowd. Now it was my turn.

As I was standing next to the podium, I could see my humble parents sitting at the table. I could feel their love and energy, and without a glitch I got close to the microphone and started my two-minute speech. Because I had practiced it so many times, I had it memorized, and because it was from my heart, I didn't need to read from a piece of paper. I gave thanks to God, President Bowen, Professor Díaz, and the university. I also made a few comments about the incredible progress that the university had made over the last decades to become a more diverse place, which had opened its doors to an immigrant student like me. I also reminded the university that there was more work to be done. Then I directed my attention to my mama and papa, and I thanked them for all their sacrifices and for making this moment possible, and then I thanked them in Spanish and told them how much I loved them. The crowd broke into a strong applause, and I said, "Thank you, thank you very much," and then I walked down the stairs and took my place next to my parents.

We hugged and cried together as my parents and the other people around the table congratulated me.

After a few moments, when it was quieter, I took the white envelope with the check and I gave it to my father and said, "Papa, please take this as my gift to you." My father opened the envelope and noticed that it was a check for nearly nine thousand dollars. As if he was holding a burning paper, he immediately closed it and gave it back to me and said, "No, son, this is your money. You worked too hard and you deserve it. It is yours." I then pushed back and put it in his hands again, and said, "No, Papa, this is for you and Mama. This is a small token of my infinite gratitude for everything that you have done and sacrificed to bring me to America, and for making this moment possible. I thank you, and I love you, and please accept this gift, Papa." My father took back the envelope. He saved it in his inner coat pocket.

This was great for them. They had been dreaming of buying their first home in America. This was enough money to complete their down payment and buy their first home. For me, this was an incredible moment of joy and of reflection. In my mind, as the celebration took place, I thought about all the obstacles that I had to overcome to get to this place, getting the highest honor at Princeton. I was also thrilled beyond belief that I was able to give back to my parents. This was one of those dreams that I carried deep in my heart, but would never share with anyone because I was afraid that they would laugh at me. As I looked around me, I could not help but recall that in this same gym, about four years before, I had raced the two-mile relay and dared to dream and, more importantly, to believe in myself. Believe that I could make things happen in my life. Now, after receiving this award, my dreams and my hopes were even higher. I was confident and full of belief that I could get into the medical school of my dreams, Harvard Medical School, and that I could one day get the honor and the privilege to help people through medicine.

I gazed once again at my humble mama. I looked into her beautiful green eyes, and I could see the reflection of our time. Those cherished memories of us laying on the green sofa as the light of the moon illuminated our house through the open patio as I learned how to read, and her words, "My love, books will change your life."

And she was right, because my love for books is what opened up infinite opportunities of adventure, exploration, and imagination. My education is what gave my family the opportunity to get our immigration status legalized and allowed me to win this amazing prize and be accepted to Harvard Medical school and MIT so that I could make my dream of helping other people through medicine a reality.

As I looked into my mother's eyes on that magical evening surrounded by the celebrations and the music and the fanfare of alumni day, I softly whispered to myself my mother's words on our green sofa, "My love, books will change your life."

"It always seems impossible until it's done."
—Nelson Mandela

"One is we should never give up. Two is you are never too old to chase your dreams. And three is it looks like a solitary sport, but it takes a team."
—Diana Nyad

My Quotes

1. *"There isn't a skill more powerful than being able to read well."*
2. *"Positive thoughts will change fear in your mind and sorrow in your heart into feelings of love, and energy, and strength."*
3. *"If you want to stand out in school, learn how to read well."*
4. *"Some of life's obstacles may seem unfair. In the long run, they will make you stronger."*
5. *"Believe or not, your parents and grandparents will give their life for you in a second."*
6. *"There isn't anything more satisfying than the power to make others feel better."*
7. *"When everything else fails, you can trust that your parents will never give up on you."*
8. *"In moments of despair and uncertainty, prayer, meditation, and reflection can bring peace."*
9. *"When you think there is no hope, it is the sweet memories of days gone by that will keep you going."*
10. *"Appreciate your parents and the simple things in life, because they may not be around forever."*
11. *"Be proud of the things that make you different. Don't allow bullying to get in your mind."*

12. *"At times, I felt as if I was trapped in a prison cell, and the walls were closing in on me."*
13. *"Find a book that speaks to you."*
14. *"No excuses. Make the best of what you have."*
15. *"Create a spark of energy. Start with a simple task but do it really well."*
16. *"You can make anything happen if you concentrate on small steps and you tackle one obstacle at a time."*
17. *"Don't be afraid to believe, it may change your life."*
18. *"Don't be afraid to dream big, despite what others might say or obstacles in front of you."*
19. *"I hope that each student graduating here tonight never gives up, for failure only exists in the mind."*
20. *"What makes you unique, is what makes you strong."*
21. *"To really fall in love with books, you need to have your own strategy that works for you."*
22. *"You see, I viewed these books as my protection. These books were my escape into a different reality."*
23. *"It's okay to cry. In fact, at some point, we all may need to cry."*
24. *"I was beginning to see that all my successes in America and my triumphs in my classes were directly related to my love for books."*
25. *"Never underestimate the pure joy of helping your parents."*

My Top List of Meaningful Quotes

Chapter 1. ***"My love, books will change your life."***
—Angela Fernandez

Chapter 2. ***"You are never too old, too wacky, too wild, to pick up a book and read, to a child."***
—Dr. Seuss

Chapter 3. ***"If you want to change the world, go home and love your family."***
—Mother Teresa

Chapter 4. ***"There are no goodbyes for us. Wherever you are, you will always be in my heart."***
—Mahatma Ghandi

Chapter 5. ***"I know from my own education that if I had not encountered two or three individuals that spent extra time with me, I would have been in jail."***
—Steve Jobs

Chapter 6. ***"Life's most persistent and urgent question is 'what are you doing for others?'"***
—Martin Luther King, Jr.

Chapter 7. ***"All you need is love."***
—The Beatles

Chapter 8. ***"First your parents, they give you your life, but then they try to give you their life."***
—Chuck Palahniuk

Chapter 9. ***"Many years later, as he faced the firing squad, Colonel Aureliano Buendia was to remember that distant afternoon when his father took him to discover ice."***
—Gabriel Garcia Marquez

Chapter 10. ***"When you wake up in the morning, think of what a privilege it is to be alive, to think, to enjoy, to love..."***
—Marcus Aurelius

Chapter 11. ***"Stay away from negative people. They have a problem for every solution."***
—Albert Einstein

Chapter 12. ***"If you are going through hell, keep going."***
—Winston Churchill

Chapter 13. ***"The greatest glory in living lies not in never falling, but in rising every time we fall."***
—Nelson Mandela

Chapter 14. ***"There are only two options: Make progress or make excuses."***
—Inky Johnson

Chapter 15. ***"The most important investment you can make is in yourself."***
—Warren Buffet

Chapter 16. ***"Passion is a choice. You need to choose to be great. It is not a chance, it's a choice."***
—Eliud Kipchoge

Chapter 17. ***"The mind is everything. What you think, you become."***
—Buddha

"You don't become what you want, you become what you believe."
—Oprah Winfrey

Chapter 18. ***"If you can dream it, you can do it."***
—Walt Disney

Chapter 19. ***"Education is the most powerful weapon which you can use to change the world."***
—Nelson Mandela

Chapter 20. ***"Everybody is a genius. But if you judge a fish by its ability to climb a tree, it will live its whole life believing that it is stupid."***
—Albert Einstein

Chapter 21. ***"Only the disciplined ones in life are free."***
—Eliud Kipchoge

"If you don't like something, change it. If you can't change it, change your attitude."
—Maya Angelou

Chapter 22. ***"You can't speed up the river and you can't slow it down; at a certain point you got to have some faith.***
—Inky Johnson

Chapter 23. ***"You must love your neighbor as yourself."***
—Jesus

Chapter 24. ***"No matter who you are or what you look like, how you started off, or how and who you love, America is a place where you can write your own destiny."***
—Barak Obama

Chapter 25. ***"It always seems impossible until it's done."***
—Nelson Mandela

"One is we should never give up. Two is you are never too old to chase your dreams. And three is it looks like a solitary sport, but it takes a team."
—Diana Nyad